T0198695

BASIC

BRAINSTORMING

THE START OF THE CREATIVE THINKING PROCESS

NEIL WUTTKE

YEAR 7 CLASSROOM TEACHER, HENLEY BEACH PRIMARY SCHOOL
DIPLOMA TEACHING, BACHELOR OF EDUCATION
CO-DIRECTOR TOURNAMENT OF MINDS, SOUTH AUSTRALIA

BALBOA.
PRESS

A DIVISION OF HAY HOUSE

Illustrations - Victoria Sears
Bachelor of Visual Communication

Balboa Press books may be ordered through booksellers or by contacting:

Balboa Press
A Division of Hay House
1663 Liberty Drive
Bloomington, IN 47403
www.balboapress.com.au
1 (877) 407-4847

ISBN: 978-1-5043-0834-2 (sc)
ISBN: 978-1-5043-0835-9 (e)

Print information available on the last page.

Balboa Press rev. date: 05/24/2017

Foreword

Brainstorming - most of us have heard of the process, but probably think we are not good at it and that others will show us up if we are involved in a group session.

This book is a guide to how anyone, child or adult, can, with practice, improve their ability to brainstorm, think divergently or think outside the square in a variety of situations.

While the book is aimed at classroom teachers who want to initiate and develop a positive process with their students, all individuals can gain from the range of these activities.

Acknowledgements/References

1. Brainstorming: Activities for Creative Thinking

    Craig Dickinson, Paula Dickinson, Eileen Rideout

    Creative Publications, 1987

2. Year Seven students at Henley Beach Primary School in Adelaide during the last few years for their creative answers.

3. www.morewords.com

4. www.enchanted learning.com.au

Brainstorming is the process of generating ideas and solutions usually within group discussions. It may be used to solve specific problems, develop new ideas, stimulate thinking or to list additional information. It can be used in a high-pressure situation or just for fun. Within a group discussion it can lead the group in many directions. Group members are encouraged to think and express ideas out loud, even if they seem to be off task, divergent or do not fit the original brief. No-one is allowed to criticise, discuss or analyse any idea until the session is deemed complete.

Brainstorming was coined by Alex Faickney Osborn (1888 – 1966) in his book

'Your Creative Power' published in 1948.

This is how he explains the name 'Brainstorming'.

'It was in 1939 when I first organised such group thinking in our company. The early participants dubbed our efforts 'Brainstorm Sessions' and quite aptly because in this case, 'brainstorm' means using the brain to storm a creative problem and do so in commando fashion, with each stormer attacking the same objective.'

Why is it effective? It can be fun and encourages creative thought and stops criticism during the group's discussions. The evaluation of the list of ideas happens later. Ideas from one group member can be built upon to make another idea or an even better idea. This can be called "piggy backing". Osborn calls this 'contagion' and 'chain reaction.' He believes that more associations are produced in groups than if one person brainstorms by themselves.

Brainstorming is like any other skill; the more you practise, the better you become. **However, some individuals, both student and adult, struggle to take an active role in these group sessions. It can be something that individuals need to learn and be confident about to be able to participate.**

This book is about how to start the creative thinking process using individuals' experiences and memories, to use their knowledge and understanding to help them to express their thoughts.

The activities in this book can help train students and adults to think for themselves and come up with multiple answers to a range of basic questions. It will also help them feel confident to participate in any group brainstorming sessions, think divergently or think outside the square. These activities can also be used to develop brain connections in people of all ages and help dementia patients to rejuvenate memory patterns.

My Experiences using Basic Brainstorming

As a classroom teacher for forty plus years, I've used brainstorming for the last twenty-six years as a daily activity called 'Peer Group Teaching' in middle primary (students from 8 to 10 years old) and upper primary (students 11 to 13 years old) classrooms in a wide variety of schools. Students are rostered on to run the session, and take control of the classroom, usually in pairs as this helps confidence. They really enjoy this level of involvement and this peer control can be a powerful tool in the classroom. One of the students asks the question, reads it twice and the class has three minutes to write down as many answers as possible.

An important step is to understand the difference between a <u>common</u> and a <u>creative</u> answer. A common answer is one that many individuals will have, but a creative answer is one that only a few will think of. I also explain that common answers are basic to the topic and obvious while a creative answer is often one step or further away from the topic and sometimes not obvious. The students gain a score by coming up with as many answers as possible within the time limit.

One point for a common answer – Three points for a creative answer

The definite three point answers are peoples' names, places, song titles (S) book titles and movie titles (M). Words that contain the smaller word are usually creative, but sometimes the word is more often than not used in a longer word. Examples of these can be seen through the book.

At the end of the time, the student running the session reads out the common answer list and the class scores their individual lists and may put one tick next to each answer that fits into this category. Next, they read out the list of the creative answers and they put three ticks next to answers that are creative. The student in control then asks for any other answers that have not been read out. They use their own judgement to decide whether it is a common answer for one point or a creative answer for three points. If a student gives an answer that has already been said they get no points, because they need to listen to other students' answers. If they piggy back their answers, I score the first two answers highly and give them one point for the rest. (Piggy backing is when they continue on with answers that are too closely related.) I often help students to decide whether the answer is worth one or three points when we first start this process. Many students are able to make this decision easily. I also like to acknowledge students who have clever answers.

Students who continually have high scores are creative thinkers. Most students will improve their score as they practise the skill on many occasions. It's often surprising the range of answers that students give. Many will have answers that you have not thought about, some will be answers from games or television shows that are currently popular.

I have listed a large selection of answers in each category but there are always more that can be added to the list.

Contents

The <u>first section</u> is on using a word in as many ways as they can. These activities encourage students to give brief answers, but to come up with as many answers as possible. Having a time limit encourages the quantity of quick answers rather than fewer detailed answers. This process develops "Fast Thinking".

The <u>second section</u> has words with a context or theme. The task is to use the category to list words within the boundaries. Words that have the same sound but different spelling can be used. (homonyms or homophones)

The <u>third section</u> requires two-part answers. This encourages student to make appropriate connections between two things, which is an essential creative thinking skill.

The <u>fourth section</u> is alphabet words. This can be used in several different forms. It can be an individual task to write down as many words as possible for each letter within the topic. Or write one word starting with the letter on the topic. It can be completed in pairs or small groups or as a competition between individuals. I have used these word lists when adults get together for a bit of fun.

Section One

1. Use the word "**back**" in as many ways as you can.

Common	Creative	
back door	back to front	piggyback
Backpack	quarterback	back stab
Backstop	back seat driver	back to school
Backache	backgammon	backside
back field	pat on the back	Nickelback
Backyard	put on the back burner	bacteria
Backhand	Jim Backus	hump back whale
Backswing	back walkover	back of the line
back stroke	*Back to the Future - M*	back in town
back stage	"Baby Come Back" - S	"Back in Black" - S
back off	back to life	"Turn Back Time" -S
backwards	I'll Be Back	Bacchus
background	back to back	
back flip	red back spider	
Backline	back in the day	
back tracking	back in time	
back down	bending over backwards	
backlash	Backstreet Boys	
	I love you to the moon and back	
	having your back to the wall	

2. Use the word "**side**" in as many ways as you can.

Common	Creative	
off side	by my side	sidestroke
leg side	sidekick	state side
side view	backside	side arm
my side	side by side	side splitter
on the side	beside	seaside
side door	inside	dark side
side dish	sideline	Homicide
side step	Far Side	upside down
sidewalk	blindsided	inside out
sideways	lighter side	right side of the law
on side	changing sides	house siding
right side	six-sided dice	outside
left side	*Westside Story - M*	consider
side show	pain in the backside	
side swipe	"Dark Side of the Moon" - S	
side of the road	Gary Sidebottom	
side saddle	"Always Look on the Bright Side of Life" - S	
side winder	"Walking side to side" - S	
	Whose side are you on?	
	cider	

3. Use the word "**front**" in as many ways as you can.

Common	Creative	
front veranda	Western front	front of house
front teeth	for front	frontal lobe
front steps	weather front	front line
front path	more front than Myer	
front room	up front	
front seat	sit down in front	
front door	fire front	
front page	front runner	
front flip	confront	
front of the line	back to front	
in front	frontal impact	
front desk	out in front	
front up	cold front	
front fence	house front	
front gate	front man	
front page	All I want for Christmas is my two front teeth	
front yard	it's just a front for the crime gang	
front wheels	final frontier	
front bumper	battlefront	

4. Use the word "**top**" in as many ways as you can.

Common	Creative	
top hat	top deck	topsy turvy
mountain top	*Top Gun -M*	on top of the world
top of class	Top Gear	long way to the top
top of fridge	top of the tree	Bottle Top Bill
top of ladder	Top Cat	make it to the top
top of building	top of the morning	pop top
top of tower	topside	top dog
top of the list	top of the wash	stop
top loader	top of food chain	
bottle top	topic	
roof top	topple	
	Hi Top	
tree top	Top Deck chocolate	
big top	top notch	
tank top	crop top	
	Tip Top	
	topping	
	Top Chief	
	"Sitting on Top of the World" - S	

5. Use the word "**base**" in as many ways as you can.

Common	Creative	
base price	basics	base running
1st base	baseball	
2nd base	base instrument	
3rd base	basement	
home base	army base	
base number	based on a true story	
base of tower	solid base	
base 10	touch base	
base ingredients	based on information	
base metal	based on facts	
base camp	base jumping	
metal base	baseline	
base of a cliff	cover all bases	
lamp base	customer base	
base step	fan base	
base floor	based on facts	
broadly based	baseman	
	database	
	wheelbase	

6. Use the word "**cover**" in as many ways as you can.

Common	Creative	
book cover	cover net	cover fire
car cover	take cover	cover drive
discover	cover up	Cover Girl Magazine
bed cover	recovery	covers
hard cover	cover letter	cover band
soft cover insurance	cover me	
cover	coverage	
pillow cover	cover version	
pool cover	drop cover roll	
	cover your work	
	WorkCover	
	take cover	
	covert operation	
	don't judge a book by its cover	
	under cover	
	look say cover write	
	Undercover Cops	
	blanket cover	
	"Cover of the Rolling Stone" - S	
	behind cover	

7. Use the word "**page**" in as many ways as you can

Common	Creative	
page of book	knight's page	Facebook page
page of history	Paige	
turn the page	pageant	
focus page	Paige Goodwin	
front page	torn page	
back page	Yellow Pages	
blank page	White Pages	
lined page	web page	
page border	home page	
read a page	pager	
A4 page	page boy	
new page	paged	
	profile page	
	Jimmy Page	
	Greg Page	
	rampage	
	slippage	
	stoppage	
	seepage	

8. Use the word "**book**" in as many ways as you can

Common	Creative	
bank book	book of matches	booked out
cheque book	Booker T Washington	*Jungle Book - M*
notebooks	bookmaker	
diaries	"Book him!"	
book report	to play by the book	
bookmark	throw the book at him	
bookmobile	book work	
book ends	book a passage on ship	
book shelf	Facebook	
book case	phone book	
books of the Bible	don't judge a book by its cover	
library book	Guinness Book of Records	
cook book	*The Notebook - M*	
book shop	Lucky Book Club	
book stand	Booker T	
booklet	Booker Boo	
address book	*The Book Thief - M*	
	Book of Eli	
	Book Week	
	bookbinding	

9. Use the word **"start"** in as many ways as you can.

Common	Creative
start a race	start again
false start	starting gun
start of the day	started
start work	startled
start the clock	start your enquiries
start the car	let's get this party started
	Star Trek - M
start test	jump start
start afresh	head start
push start	restart
start school	starting point
stop start	start the car
	start to finish
	Homestart
	kick start
	nonstarter
	upstart
	starters
	start up

10. Use the word **"end"** in as many ways as you can.

Common	Creative	
end of the rope	end to end	fend off
end of the race	this is the end	mend
end of track	Living End	vending machine
end of the day	end of the road	end of the world
the end	*End of Days - M*	the end is nigh
Mile End	endless	depend
	ending	friend
	Endless Summer - M	
	to the bitter end	
	beginning of the end	
	Never Ending Story -M	
	dead end	
	endurance	
	endoscopy	
	reach the end of the line	
	book ends	
	send	
	trend	
	bend	

11. Use the word "**hook**" in as many ways as you can.

Common	Creative	
fish hook	let off the hook	hookworm
barbed hook	hook, line and sinker	tenterhooks
hook on the wall	Captain Hook	
hook you in	by hook or crook	
coat hook	Sky Hooks	
key hook	Velcro hook	
	Hook - M	
	shook	
	hooked	
	hooked on you	
	"Hooked on a Feeling" - S	
	chook	
	right hook	
	hooky	
	hooking	
	hooker	
	hook up	
	L J Hooker	

12. Use the word "**line**" in as many ways as you can.

Common	Creative
dotted lines	headlines
four-square lines	guidelines
waiting in line	airlines
line up	ocean liners
cross the line	line backer
clothes line	football line
deadline	toe the line
fishing line	walk the line
eye liner	borderline
coastline	finish line
number line	white line fever
line drawn on paper	silver lining
	read between the lines
	"Blurred Lines" - S
	Madeline -M
	dateline
	help line
	police line up
	line dance

13. Use the word "**net**" in as many ways as you can.

Common	Creative	
basketball net	Cornett	The Netherlands
hockey net	double net	New Jersey Nets
volley ball net	cabinet	Craig Nettles
tennis net	fish net stockings	Internet
insect net	safety net	Annette
butterfly net	netball	net of a solid
cargo net	Netflix	
hair net	Brooklyn Nets	
	network	
	stinging nettle	
	netting magnet	
	bonnet	
	Antoinette	
	cornet	
	hornet	
	phonetics	
	spinet piano	
	net profile	
	security net	

14. Use the word "**fish**" in as many ways as you can.

Common	Creative	
fishing rod	sufficient	fish for clues
fishing line	fish finder	Fisher Price
fish and chips	fish song	fishy
fish cakes	sleeping with the fish	Fish Avenue
go fishing	fish out of water	fisher
fishing boat	Rainbow Fish	fisheries
fishing trawler	fish legs	I Fish
cat fish	*Fish Called Wanda - M*	
fishing spot	fisherman	Fisher and Paykel
fish scales	goldfish	school of fish
fishing book	silverfish	
fish shop	fishing for likes	
fish bait	Michael Fisher	
fish bowl	fishing charter	
fish tank	fishmonger	
fish sauce	fishery	
fish clown	gone fishing	
puffer fish	worst day fishing is better than best day working	

15. Use the word "**rod**" in as many ways as you can.

Common	Creative	
fishing rod	product	produce
lightning rod	Rod Stewart	pushrod
reinforcing rod	rod for my back	
steel rod	rodent	
wooden rod	rode	
	rode on horse	
	hot rod	
	Brodie	
	rodeo	
	rudder	
	Rod Laver	
	Rodney	
	Rodger	
	Rodger Rabbit - M	
	ram rod	
	aerodrome	
	by product	
	electrode	
	erode	

16. Use the word "**silver**" in as many ways as you can.

Common	Creative
silver coin	Long John Silver
silver tray	silverback
silver dollar	Hi Ho Silver
silver spoon	*Silver Streak - M*
silver paint	quicksilver
silver bullet	silverware
silver star	
silver mine	silver ingot
silver wedding	sterling silver
silver anniversary	stars of the silver screen
silverfish	100% pure silver
silver taste	Silvery
silver medal	silversmith
gold and silver	born with a silver spoon in their mouth
silver cup	

17. Use the word "**gold**" in as many ways as you can.

Common	Creative	
gold coins	Golden Retriever	Golden Crumpets
gold fillings	Goldie Hawn	golden bird
gold mine	Golda Meir	Goldilocks
gold plate	marigold	
goldsmith	goldenrod	
gold dust	The Golden Rule	
gold doubloons	Golden Gate Bridge	
gold digger	a heart of gold	
gold medal	band of gold	
gold bracelet	*Goldfinger - M*	
gold necklace	golden ticket - Willy Wonka	
gold star	Golden Arches McDonalds	
	Black and Gold	
	Golden Labrador	
	Golden Gaytime	
	black gold	
	gold rush	
	golden geese	
	gold fish	

18. Use the word "**red**" in as many ways as you can.

Common	Creative	
red scarf	redback	*Red October - M*
red pencil	Red Cross	"Red Red Wine" - S
red paint	Little Red Riding Hood	Red Dwarf
red book	red carpet	Red Baron
red ball	*Drop Dead Fred - M*	red alert
red wall	Red Rock Deli	red flag
red light	shred	Red Bull
redhead	*Red Dog - M*	run a red light
red face	ruby red slippers	redeem
redgum	big red car	Fred
	big red ball	red as a beetroot
	roses are red	Boston Red Socks
	credit	
	Big Red Predator	
	redneck	
	Redding	
	Red Symonds	
	Clifford the Big Red Dog	
	"Rudolph the Red Nosed Reindeer" - S	

19. Use the word "**blue**" in as many ways as you can.

Common	Creative	
bright blue	Blue Poles	
aqua blue	Blue Ray	blue bird
light blue	blue screen	Blue Heeler
blue sky	"Blue Sky Mining" - S	Jim Blue
blue pen	got the blues	big blue sea
blue paint	Blue Loo	
blue Texta	"Singing the Blues" - S	
blue car	Double Blues	
blue eyes	Little boy blue	
blue lips	"Baby's got Blue Eyes" - S	
blue eyeshadow	blue water fishing	
blue water	out of the blue	
navy blue	*Blue Hawaii - M*	
royal blue	Mr Blue Sky	
	black and blue	
	"Blue Suede Shoes" -S	
	blue ring octopus	
	Blue Illusion	
	blue on blue	

20. Use the word "**green**" in as many ways as you can.

Common	Creative	
light green	Green Arrow	greenkeeper
dark green	Green Lantern	golf green
lime green	Green Hornet	Green Party
green pen	green thumb	Green Day
green paint	Jolly Green Giant	Greenback
green Texta	green with envy	Greenland
green eyes	green around the gills	greenhouse
green car	Lorne Green	
green slime	Al Green	
green jelly beans	Greenhills Adventure Park	
green Smarties	Rachel Green	
green M&M's	"Green Grow the Rushes O" - S	
green Tic Tacs	greener on the other side	
green apple	Where is the Green Sheep?	
	Green Bean Café	
	greenhouse gasses	
	Greenwich Mean Time	
	Green Eggs and Ham - M	
	"Green, Green Grass of Home" - S	

21. Use the word **"finger"** in as many ways as you can.

Common	Creative	
index finger	Scotch Fingers	pull my finger
ring finger	butter fingers	
pointer finger	*Gold Finger - M*	
little finger	finger puppet	
finger exercises	give the finger	
finger width	fingernails	
long fingers	fingerprints	
short fingers	light fingers	
rude finger	cheese fingers	
tapping fingers	finger food	
drumming fingers	fish fingers	
broken finger	Finger Lick'n Good	
pinkie finger	five finger discount	
salad fingers	finger bun	
	fingers do the walking	
	put your finger in your ear	
	point your finger	
	fingerless gloves	
	finger on the pulse	

22. Use the word **"hand"** in as many ways as you can.

Common	Creative	
dominant hand	handicap	handle
backhand	handcuff	hands high
hands up	hand to hand combat	hand in mine
hand out	put left hand in	handball
handmaid	give me a hand	right hand man
hand pass	many hands make light work	
handwriting	Han Dynasty	talk to the hand
hand wash	handshake	Chandler
clock hands	hand me downs	caught red handed
handspring	Edward Scissor Hands	handyman
left hand	keep my hands to myself	
right hand	first hand	Cool Hand Luke
big hands	second hand	hands up in the air
hand span	helping hand	
hand dryer	hand it to them	
hand towel	"Hands Across the Water" - S	
hand gun	don't bite the hand that feeds you	
	"I Want to Hold your Hand" - S	
	handful	

23. Use the word "foot" in as many ways as you can.

Common	Creative	
small foot	bare foot	footy
wide foot	football	foot of bed
short foot	one foot in front of the other	
foot massage	Bigfoot	foothills
foot rub	foot the bill	football cards
foot spa	footpath	Footy Show
arch your foot	footprint	
foot smell	foot step	
cold foot	Foot Long sub	
right foot	best foot forward	
left foot	Footlocker	
	Australian Football League	
	Footloose - M	
	athletes foot	
	header and footer	
	put your left foot in	
	footage	
	foot and mouth disease	
	foot in the door	

24. Use the word "arm" in as many ways as you can.

Common	Creative	
left arm	arm wrestle	armed, arm yourself
right arm	brothers in arms	firearm
arm's length	Prince Charming	armed truck
arm's width	Lance Armstrong	armour
armful	Neil Armstrong	Army, armies
arm rest	coat of arms	link arms
armchair	arms race	Armadale
broken arm	nuclear arms	arm in arm
overarm	Marmite	right arm of the law
underarm	alarm clock	long arm of the law
forearm	knight's armour	armadillo
arms	strong arm	*Armageddon - M*
	Armor All	harm, warm
	karma	harmony
	Carmel	alarm
	Garmin	farm
	Farmer's Market	balmy night
	Carmichael	parmy
	armpit	Parmesan cheese

25. Use the word "**leg**" in as many ways as you can.

Common	Creative	
chair leg	leg room	legal
table leg	legacy	legless
broken leg	bootlegger	legume
chicken leg	no leg to stand on	red legs
pants leg	on one's last legs	telegraph
leg of lamb	last leg of relay race	
centipede's legs	shake a leg	
first leg	pulling your leg	
leg up	leg work	
	Lego's pasta	
	leg it	
	Lego	
	break a leg	
	a lot of leg work	
	three-legged race	
	allege	
	college	
	elegant	
	illegal	

26. Use the word "**eye**" in as many ways as you can.

Common	Creative	
fish eye	see the whites of your eye	
black eye	*Eye of the Tiger - M*	conveyed
two eyes	Black Eyed Peas	deadeye
blue eyes	eye of the storm	eyeliner
green eyes	Popeye	eyesore
brown eyes	the eyes have it	eyeteeth
cross eyed	real eye opener	tiger eyes
eye patch	keep an eye on them	
eye glasses	I Spy with My Little Eye	
eye glass	Hawkeye	
red eyes	Ten Eyewitness News	
eyelash	bullseye	
eyebrow	eye on the prize	
eye liner	"Baby's Got Blue Eyes" - S	
watery eyes	got my eye on you	
eyeshadow	bloodshot eyes	
	I can see it in your eyes	
	all seeing eye	
	birds eye	

27. Use the word "**ear**" in as many ways as you can.

Common	Creative	
ear muffs	fear	gear
earring	hear	bear
ear wax	dear	year
ear drum	near	pear
ear lobe	tear	
thick ear	lend an ear	
pierced ear	ear to ear	
swollen ear	good ear	
red ear	ear infection	
ear hole	perforated ear drum	
ear piercing	are your ears painted on	
	Goldilocks and the Three Bears	
	ear to the ground	
	eyes and ears and mouth and nose	
	Cameron Gear	
	earphones	
	cheers big ears	
	beard	

28. Use the word "**nose**" in as many ways as you can.

Common	Creative	
big nose	nose bleed section	hardnose
runny nose	on the nose	nosebleeds
sunburnt nose	stick your nose in it	nosedive
blood nose	pick your nose	nosepiece
broken nose	win by a nose	
pointy nose	stop nosing about	
	nosey parker	
	nose job	
	up your nose with a rubber hose	
	don't cut off your nose to spite your face	
	"Rudolph the Red Nosed Reindeer" - S	
	"Eyes and Ears and Mouth and Nos" - S	
	plain as the nose on your face	
	Mr Big Nose	
	keep your nose out	
	got your nose	
	Mr Nosy	
	brown nose	
	diagnose	

29. Use the word "**mouth**" in as many ways as you can.

Common	Creative	
wide mouth	loud mouth	goalmouth
big mouth	mouth of cave	mouthful
open mouth	mouth of river	mouthpiece
full mouth	mouth to mouth resuscitation	
	Wide Mouth Frog	
	mouth of the woods	
	mouthguard	
	out of the mouths of babes	
	shut your mouth; you look like a fish	
	wash your mouth out with soap	
	close your mouth when eating	
	keep your mouth shut	
	Luna Park mouth	
	mouthorgan	
	mouth of the south	
	Murray Mouth	
	blabber mouth	
	Ralph Mouth	
	badmouth	

30. Use the word "**head**" in as many ways as you can.

Common		Creative	
air head	pot heads	header	heads and tails
bald head	knucklehead	ahead of the pack	headless
big head	hit your head	headache	headspace
broom head	red head	beheaded	in over your head
head height	saw head	bighead	lose your head
head home	small head	boof head	off with your head
head lice	warhead	egg head	headliner
broom head	head wear	eyes in the back of my head	
head height		head band	war heads
head lights		head banger	headmaster
head nurse		head butt	Headingly
head of faculty		head down under	skinhead
head of school		headlights	head phones
head out		head of company	head the wrong way
head shape		head of the river	head waiter
head space		head of the school	headstrong
headless		head over heels	headless horseman
headless chook		heads down, thumbs up	
heads up		Head tennis racquets	

31. Use the word "**rock**" in as many ways as you can.

Common	Creative	
rock pool	Red Rock Chips	Ayres Rock
big rock	*Camp Rock - M*	Chris Rock
small rock	Rock N Roll	
flat rock	Hard Rock Café	
round rock	Hard Rock ride	
bedrock	The Big Rocking Horse	
rock wall	rocky road	
garden rocks	don't rock the boat	
landscaping rocks	Canadian Rockies	
	"Rock around the Clock" - S	
	skimming rocks	
	solid as a rock	
	Flat Rock	
	Rocky - M	
	rock star	
	rocking horse	
	rocking chair	
	pocket rocket	
	rock bottom	

32. Use the work "**block**" in as many ways as you can.

Common		Creative	
around the block	block of flats	H & R Block	Mega block
block of land	wooden blocks	block and tackle	building blocks of life
block letter		Block Island	roadblock
block of chocolate		Blockhead	
block of ice		a block of time	
block of wood		The Block	
blockade		choc a block	
blockage		Blockbusters	
building blocks		block word	
cement block		jog around the block	
football blocker		sun block	
ice block		block head	
lap of the block Lego		blocked toilet	
block		blocked drain	
glass block		mental block	
unblock		block website	
to block traffic		blockbuster	
toilet block		new kids on the block	
		a block away	

33. Use the work **"brick"** in as many ways as you can.

Common	Creative
brick wall	bric a brac
bricklayer	as heavy as a brick
brick phone	Yellow Brick Road
brick house	Lego brick
brick path	Three Little Pig bricks
red brick	brick kiln
black brick	"Just Another Brick in the Wal"l -S
brickie	What do you have in that backpack? Bricks?
bricks	thick as a brick
stack of bricks	Brickworks
brick paving	brickbats
brick floors	brickyard
	fire bricks
	brick bat

34. Use the word **"wall"** in as many ways as you can.

Common	Creative	
timber wall	Wallenberg	Wallspan
brick wall	David Wall	walled city
stone wall	Wall Mart wall climb	
castle wall	The Great Wall of China	
plaster wall	just another brick in the wall	
sea wall	Walls of Jericho	
garden wall	Wall of Fame	
rock wall	Berlin Wall	
	Wallis theatre	
	Wallis and Grommet	
	wallaroo	
	Where's Wally?	
	wallpaper	
	bang your head against a brick wall	
	Whispering Wall	
	"Wonder Wall" - S	
	Wally World	
	wallet	
	Wally Lewis	

35. Use the word "**sand**" in as many ways as you can.

Common	Creative	
sand box	sandwich	sandbags
sand pit	sandals	thousand
sand castles	Sandman	sandblast
sand paper	Carl Sandburg's poetry	
sand trap	Sandinistas	
sand bags	San Diego	
sand painting	a thousand	
beach sand	Sandy	
sand dunes	quick sand	
sand hill	hour glass	
white sand	white sand	
brick sand	"Look at me I'm Sandra Dee" - S	
washed sand	sands of time	
soft sand	sandcastles	
desert sand	sand sculptures	
hot sand	Sandra	
	sanding	
	Golden Sands	

36. Use the word "**dog**" in as many ways as you can.

Common	Creative	
dog bowl	hot dog	In the dog house
dog lead	sick as a dog	D for dog
dog biscuits	doggone	doggy bag
dog whistle	Deputy Dog	dog paddle
dog kennel	seeing eye dog	
dog breeds	dog rescue	
dog muzzle	guide dog	
barking dog	raining cats and dogs	
bulldog	"Who let the Dogs Out" - S	
dog paddle	*Dog Day Afternoon - M*	
puppy dog eyes	Snoop Dog	
dog with a bone	Clifford the Big Red Dog	
	Red Dog - M	
	Western Bulldogs	
	sausage dog	
	British Bulldog	
	corn dog	
	Cats vs Dogs - M	
	underdog	

37. Use the word "**cat**" in as many ways as you can.

Common	Creative	
cat bowl	Top Cat	cat got your tongue
cat box	catnap	*Cats and Dogs - M*
cat breed	caterpillar	catacombs
annoying cat	Catalina Island	cat on a hot tin roof
cat tray	catastrophe	catering
cat eyes	wild cat	bob cat
	raining cats and dogs	Kathmandu
	Cat in the Hat	Garfield the cat
	cattle	cattle
	Cat Empire	
	cat o nine tails	
	Aristocats - M	
	scatter	
	catfish	
	catwalk	
	cats have nine lives	
	cat and mouse	
	meerkat	
	Kit Kat	

38. Use the word "**horse**" in as many ways as you can.

Common	Creative	
horse breed	hobby horse	work horse
horse racing	horsing around	horse and carriage
racehorse	saw horse	horse and buggy
rocking horse	hoarse voice	
horse saddle	horse power	
horse manure	Horseshoe Bay	
	horse-fly	
	Headless Horseman	
	horseshoe	
	sea horse	
	Four Horsemen of the Apocalypse - M	
	big as a horse	
	lucky horse shoe	
	Trojan Horse - M	
	war horse	
	A horse is a horse of course of course	
	Big Rocking Horse	
	all the king's horses	
	from the horse's mouth	

39. Use the word "**bird**" in as many ways as you can.

Common	Creative	
bird bath	Tweety Bird	
bird cage	a bird in the hand	birds and bees
bird feeder	Big Bird	song bird
bird seed	Bird Man	bird flu
bird hide	Bird in Hand	bye bye birdie
bird perch	birdie in golf	bird dance
	bird brain	
	Bird Man of Alcatraz - M	
	Larry Bird basketballer	
	birds of a feather flock together	
	"Bird, Bird, Bird, Bird is the Word" - S	
	Bird on a Wire - M	
	A little bird told me	
	Angry Birds	
	she's a top bird	
	It's a bird, it's a plane, it's Superman	
	blackbird	
	bird's eye	
	bird's eye view	

40. Use the word "**duck**" in as many ways as you can.

Common	Creative	
domestic duck	duck your head duckling	
sitting duck	Aquaduck toilet cleaner ducktails	
duck pond	duck down	duckweed
dead duck	Pluck a Duck	duck walk
Three Little Ducks	Donald Duck	
ducky	Daffy Duck	
rubber ducky	ugly duckling	
duck sign	duck dive	
	Duck Duck Goose	
	"he ducked his head umpire"	
	"Three Little Ducks" - S	
	duck whistle	
	The Ducksters - M	
	Sarah and Duck	
	Golden Duck	
	Peking Duck	
	duck for cover	
	duck curry	
	duckbill	

41. Use the word "**age**" in as many ways as you can.

Common	Creative	
old age	agent	footage
teenage	agency	bandage
Prehistoric Age	you've been gone for ages	
middle age	Age of Empires onstage	
underage	usage	engage
Atomic Age	garage	damage
ageless	stage	garbage
Stone Age	wage	image
Ice Age	sage	cage
	cottage	
	page	
	rage	
	Ice Age - M	
	advantage	
	agenda	
	birdcage	
	mileage	
	luggage	
	corkage	

42. Use the word "**year**" in as many ways as you can.

Common	Creative	
Year 1	as the years pass by	midyear
Year 2	yearling	yearly
Year 3	Year 7 graduation	yearning
Year 4	Year 12 graduation	Happy New Year
Year 5	yearly	
Year 6	New Year's Eve	
Year 7	Year of the Monkey	
Year 8	new year - new me	
Year 9	100 Years	
Year 10	leap year	
Year 11	yesteryear	
Year 12	Buzz Lightyear	
New Year	gap year	
year book	three year warranty	
this year	employee of the year	
last year	until the year ends	
once a year	Goodyear	
	mark of the year	
	Book of the Year	

43. Use the word "young" in as many ways as you can.

Common	Creative
young lady	young and beautiful
young man	night is still young
young thing	The Young Ones
five year's young	Neil Young
young animal	Ernest Young
young love	Forever Young
young baby	Young Talent Time
	Young Dracula - M
	"Young Wild and Free" - S
	The Young and the Restless
	Young Justice
	Johnny Young
	Maddy Young
	Aaron Young
	youngster
	the night is still young
	younger

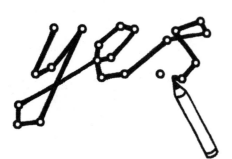

44. Use the word "old" in as many ways as you can.

Common	Creative	
five years old	Old Noarlunga	olden days
how old?	out with the old	old dogs
old bike	I'm too old for this	old school
old man	Old Kent Road	sold
old car	"Grand Old Duke of York" - S	
Old Port Road	marigold	told
Golden Grove	old English cheese	hold
little old lady	old folks' home	bold
hot and cold	cold fridge	cold
old gum tree	Goldilocks	fold
old tricks	Holden	golden oldie
	Gary Oldman	gold digger
		Golden Gate Bridge
	Golden North Ice Cream *Gold Finger* - M	
	"Old Man River" - S	Cold Rock
	Mt Bold Reservoir	scold
	you can't teach an old dog new tricks	
	The Bold and the Beautiful	
	Golden Grove	

45. Use the word "**baby**" in as many ways as you can.

Common	Creative
baby room	"Baby Did a Bad Bad Thing" - S
baby boy	Million Dollar Baby - M Babies Are Us
baby girl	"Rock a Bye Baby" - S stop babying
baby animal	baby cakes Babylon
baby sister	Baby Baby - S Babybel Cheese
baby brother	"Don't Leave Me Baby"- S
baby pram	Babysit
baby clothes	Ice, Ice Baby - S
baby names	"Baby's Got Blue Eyes" - S
baby teeth	My Baby Bunting
newborn baby	baby shower
	baby blue
	baby boomer
	sugar baby
	jelly babies
	baby grand
	baby back ribs
	Baby's Day Out - M
	Baby Born

46. Use the word "**short**" in as many ways as you can.

Common	Creative	
short stuff	shorts	shortly
short ball	shortening	shortcut
short circuit	short end of the stick	shortcake
short stop	Short Hand Luke	short come
short wave radio	Get Shorty - M	short sighted
short hair	being short with someone	
	the long and short of it	
	short man syndrome short	
	of funds	
	shortly	
	come up short shortbread	
	shortage	
	short changed	
	shorten	
	shortfall	
	shortstop	
	shortwave	
	shorthand	

47. Use the word "**long**" in as many ways as you can.

Common	Creative
long division	oblong longbow
long shot	belong longest
long johns	"Long and Winding Road" - S
long stemmed roses	furlong longitude
long distance	long way home Oblong
long hair	Long Island NY longhorn
long winded	longshoreman yearlong
long ago	longitude prolong
long way	General Longstreet
	Texas Longhorns
	Henry Wadsworth Longfellow
	long way down
	daddy long legs
	Long John Silver
	long and the short of it
	long long time ago
	along
	headlong
	lifelong

48. Use the word "**high**" is as many ways as you can.

Common	Creative
high chair	high hat hold your head high
high mountain	*High School Musical* – M highway robbery
high jump	get off your high horse
high rise building	high hat drums
high roof	*Sky High - M*
high table	high five
high bar	Hi Five
high school	thigh
sugar high	high street
high blood pressure	highway
high speed	highway to hell
high cloud	my way or the highway
	The Block – Sky High
	Flying High -M
	Summer Heights High
	high noon
	Blue Water High
	Harry Highpants
	interstate highway
	High Wide and Handsome

49. Use the word "**low**" in as many ways as you can.

Common	Creative	
low table	How low can you go?	blowing wind
low chair	a low front	Lindsay Lohan
low bridge	low life	Light and Low
low down	low down	slow
low rider	hollow	glow
low ceiling	lower	blow
low roof	glow	slow down
low branch	flow	slow up
low score	lower deck	
low level	lowering	
low lying	glow worm	
low tide	slow and steady	
low cost	glower	
low pitched noise	go slow	
low gear	Lowes clothing	
low key	below	
	lower the boom	
	"Swing Low Sweet Chariot" - S	
	"Blowing in the Wind" - S	

50. Use the word "**tall**" in as many ways as you can.

Common	Creative	
tall person	taller	tallyho
tall glass	tallest	vitally
tall building	stall	totally
tall tree	stalling	stallholder
tall shelf	install	tallies
tall seat	installed	
tall table	installation	
	installing	
	tall tale	
	standing tall	
	tall poppy syndrome	
	tally	
	Tally ho!	
	tallest to smallest	
	bookstall	
	fatally	
	installer	
	metallic	
	mentally	

51. Use the word "talk" in as many ways as you can.

Common	Creative	
talk back	talk show	talking under water
talking	talk back radio	Talking Heads
talk a lot	small talk	Jack and Beanstalk
pep talk	stalk	If the walls could talk
talk to the hand	stalking	talk too much
trash talk	talk over the top	
talk is cheap	"Jive Talking" - S	
	talk the talk	
	"We Don't Talk Anymore" - S	
	smooth talker	
	talk with silver tongue	
	stop talking	
	continuous talking	
	nonstop talking	
	pillow talk	
	don't talk with your food in your mouth	
	talk with a mouth full of marbles	
	Talk to the Animals - M	
	walkie talkie	

52. Use the word "call" in as many ways as you can.

Common	Creative
call out	called
call centre	caller
phone call	carpet call
loud call	Callum
video call	call of nature
Skype call	call of the wild
recall	one call away
recalled	callus
called in	*Call of Duty - M*
	Call the Midwife
	calligraphy
	calligraphy writing
	calligrapher
	calligraphic
	call for help
	Callington
	"I Just Called to Say I Love You" - S
	"Ring Ring Why Don't You Give Me a Call" - S
	"Who You Gonna Call? Ghostbusters" - S

53. Use the word "**ring**" in as many ways as you can.

Common	Creative
diamond ring	bring
ring tone	"You Can Ring My Bell" - S
wedding ring	Ring of Confidence
friendship ring	Ring, Ring - S
engagement ring	5 gold rings
gymnastics rings	"Ring a Ring a Rosy" - S
O ring	*Lord of the Rings - M*
ringlets	Olympic rings
mood ring	Burger Rings
hearing	onion rings
ring leader	"Put a Ring on It" - S
	Pringles
	wrestling ring
	fringe
	ring the door bell
	Ringo Starr
	blue ringed octopus
	bring it on
	string

54. Use the word "**bell**" in as many ways as you can.

Common	Creative
school bell	*For Whom the Bell Tolls - M*
cow bell	Bells Beach
lunch bell	"Ring My Bell" - S
recess bell	Bella
home bell	Liberty Bell
bell monitor	John Bell
warning bell	Anabelle
bell lap	Bela Lugosi
delivery bell	Bellchambers
bell tower	belle of the ball
	belly button
	blacksmith's bellows
	Tinker Bell
	"Jingle Bells" - S
	bluebells
	bellowed
	Taco Bell
	Alexander Graham Bell
	"Oranges and Lemons Say the Bells of St Clements" - S

55. Use the word "**buzz**" in as many ways as you can.

Common	Creative
any insect	buzzard
mosquito buzz	buzz a field in a plane
buzz saw	buzz cut
alarm clock buzz	give him a buzz
bees buzz	buzz off
	Buzz Game
	Buzz Lightyear
	buzzer
	abuzz
	buzzer
	buzzword
	buzzing sound

56. Use the word "**jump**" in as many ways as you can.

Common	Creative
jump rope	Jump Rope for Heart
jump up	jumper
jump down	jump suit
jump around	jumper cables
jump on board	jump start
jump down	jump the gun
jump over	jump right in
jump in	"Jump on Board" -S
	hop skip jump
	I Can Jump Puddles
	Jumping Jacks
	"Jumping Jack Flash" -S
	21 Jump Street
	Jolly Jumper
	outjump
	when I say jump, you say how high
	jumps

57. Use the word "**hop**" in as many ways as you can.

Common	Creative	
on the hop	hop scotch	lamb chop
hop down	hip hop	lolly shop
hop up	hop skip jump	Shaver Shop
hop along	hop along	whopper
hop out	hops beer	Big Whopper
hop in	Denis Hopper	
hop on	hopeless	
	hop to it	
	shop	
	shopping	
	hope	
	hopeful	
	hippity hop	
	hop on board	
	Hoppo Bumpo	
	hopper	
	chopper	
	grasshopper	
	Hopalong Cassidy	

58. Use the word "**run**" in as many ways as you can.

Common	Creative	
fun run	crunch	strung
run over	brunch	prunes
run on	Game of Thrones	runes
run off	run the gauntlet	City to Bay Run
runners	running from the law	run in your stocking
run away	on the run	Maze Runner - M
morning run	Runaway - M	runaway train
cross country run	runny nose	Chicken run - M
run a red light	Mother's Day Run	trundle wheel
100m run	runt	Road Runner
	colour run	better run
	Running of the Bulls	Run Forest run
	Rundle	Cool Runnings - M
	Rundle Street	Riverrun
	Rundle Mall	
	feeling run down	
	Runaway Birds	
	running late	
	Running Man Challenge	

59. Use the word "**fly**" in as many ways as you can.

Common	Creative	
blow fly	fly blown	when pigs fly
tent fly	Marty McFly	Royal Flying doctor
baseball fly	flying saucer	*Flying High - M*
fly away	butterfly	
fly on a plane	horse fly	
flying fish	dragon fly	
buzz off fly	march fly	
your fly is undone	sand fly	
	fly Emirates	
	on the fly	
	lady bird, fly away home	
	flying holiday	
	Louis the Fly	
	Flybuys Card	
	These Wings Are Made to Fly	
	fly in the ointment	
	fly off the handle	
	Too Fly for a White Guy - M	
	"Shoo Fly Don't Bother Me" - S	

60. Use the word "**step**" in as many ways as you can.

Common	Creative	
front step	footsteps	Stepathon
back step	step on down	
step up	one step at a time	
step down	follow the steps	
step aboard	Stepney	
step mum	step in time	
step dad	next step	
step brother	step on it	
step sister	stepping stones	
step family	step up to the plate	
dance steps	stepping in netball	
step forward	spring in my step	
	step up to the challenge	
	watch your step	
	One small step for man one giant leap for mankind	
	one small step at a time	
	step in the right direction	
	two steps forward, one step back	

61. Use the word "**hot**" in as many ways as you can.

Common		Creative	
hot day	hot curry	hot on the trail	Hot Wheels
hot night		hot on the heels	hot cakes
hot chocolate		telephone hotline	gun shot
hot dog		hotel	hot price
hot food		"Hotel California" - S	looking hot
hot air balloon		Grand Hotel	hot sale
hot cross buns		*Odd Angry Shot - M*	Hotmail
hot potato		hot property	shot
hot rod		"It's Getting Hot in Here" - S	
hot rocks		"Hot August Night" - S	shot in the dark
hot ate		"Feeling Hot Hot Hot" -S	hot property
hot fudge		"Hot Potato" - S	
hot drink		great shot	
hot water		hotel counter	
hot temperature		hotel booking	
hot sauce		hotel room	
hot weather		"Hot in the City" - S	
hot sun		hotel porter	
hot chilli		hotel concierge	

62. Use the word "**cold**" in as many ways as you can.

Common	Creative	
cold fridge	scold	cold room
cold drink	scolded	ice cold
cold temperature	cold blooded	Cold Rock
common cold	out in the cold	Coldplay
cold heart	cold cuts	
cold climate	Cold War	
cold weather	cold shoulder	
cold water	cold case	
	cold and flu tablets	
	"Baby it's Cold Outside" - S	
	trail has gone cold	
	Mr Cold	
	cold start	
	It's Cold in Here	
	cold rolls	
	cold sore	
	"Cold as Ice" - S	
	hurry up or your food will go cold	
	only thing you can catch is a cold	

LOADING IDEAS

63. Use the word "day" in as many ways as you can.

Common		Creative	
bad day	good day	Holiday	birthday party
long day		daybreak	365 days a year
today		daydream	yesterday
daylight		Daydream Island	olden days
day in court		New Year's Day	g'day
great day		Days of Our Lives	doomsday
sunny day		Heyday	good old days
next day		D-Day	Mother's Day
Monday		"Hard Day's Night" - S	Father's Day
Tuesday		a day in the life of	It's Friday
Wednesday		"Daydream Believer" - S	public holiday
Thursday		casual clothes day Today Tonight	
Friday		*Day of the Triffids - M*	Daya
Saturday		Days Hire	Valentine's Day
Sunday		Jason Day	Green Day
Gala Day		day/night chemist birthday	
one day		*Independence Day - M* Happy Days	
day time		"Those were the Days" – S Australia Day	
day light		Hey Hey it's Saturday *Daddy Day Care - M*	

64. Use the word "**night**" in as many ways as you can.

Common	Creative	
night light	nightgown	once a night
goodnight	night fall	
night terrors	nightmares	
night fright	Nightingale	
last night	night club	
night time	*Dark was the Night - M*	
good night	Gladys Knight	
tomorrow night	Peter Knight	
	Knights of the Round Table	
	white knight	
	knight	
	night spot	
	Black Night - S	
	Night Moves	
	Last Night -S	
	"Knights in White Satin" - S	
	big night out	
	"Blame it on the Night"- S	
	Knights Templar	

32

65. Use the word "fire" in as many ways as you can.

Common	Creative	
house fire	Fireman Sam	bushfire front
camp fire	fireman	Set Fire to the Rain
on fire	ready aim fire	bushfire season
fire engine	getting fired	contained fire
fire truck	you're fired	firearm
gas fire	Fire Fire Fire	fire extinguisher
wood fire	Light My Fire -S	fireflies
toxic fire	Earth Wind and Fire	firework
grass fire	Fire in the Hole	Goblet of Fire
	fire up	"Just Like Fire" -S
	"Fire and Rain" - S	backfire
	"We Didn't Start the Fire" - S	
	you're on fire	catch on fire
	fire when ready	fire ants
	set on fire	fire bug
	Fire of London	fire hydrant
	"This Girl is on Fire" -S	ceasefire
	fire wall	
	Fire Boy and Water Girl	

66. Use the word "in" in as many ways as you can.

Common	Creative	
inside	in the dog house	Tin Tin
in your seat	money in the bank tin	
in tune	wolf in sheep's clothing bin	
in trouble	stuck in the mud	sin
in love	pain in the neck	mine
in training	made in Australia	shine
in the past	fin	twine
tucked in	inside out	swine
	snake in the grass	
	down in the dumps	
	mother in law	
	brother in law	
	in between	
	intercept	
	included	
	ring	
	Institute	
	inspect	
	inconsistent	

67. Use the word "**out**" in as many ways as you can.

Common	Creative	
out to lunch	you're out	gout
out of your depth	out and about	bout
lights out	out in the cold	spout
out played	out of business	snout
out gunned	outboard	pout
out talked	outboard motor	stand about
	died out	out of time
	outer space	out of bounds
	outback Australia	down and out
	out fielders	"Out of my Head" - S
	outlaws	family outings
	outstanding	Outlander
	shout	outrage
	lout	work this out
	in and out	
	outdoors	
	router	
	outside	
	inside out	

68. Use the word "**whole**" in as many ways as you can.

Common	Creative
whole milk	wholesale
whole number	buying wholesale
whole thing	whole world
eat it whole	wholly involved
whole of the point	"Whole World in His Hands" - S
whole lot of trouble	wholesome
	"Whole Lot of Something Going On" - S
	wholegrain
	wholemeal
	wholemeal bread
	whole leaf
	wholefood
	"It's a Whole New World" - S

69. Use the word "**hole**" in as many ways as you can.

Common	Creative	
make a hole	whole	manhole
dig a hole	hole in the floor	posthole
drill a hole	hole in the roof	buttonhole
hole saw	"Hole in My Bucket" - S	pinhole
golf hole	hole in one	peephole
bolt hole	fell in a hole	sinkhole
ear hole	hole in the boat	
mouth hole	rabbit hole	
	fox hole	
	ant hole	
	fixing a hole	
	black hole	
	Holes Book	
	shut your pie hole	
	eat it whole	
	whole lot of trouble	
	In the hole	
	blowhole	
	loophole	

70. Use the word "**half**" in as many as you can.

Common	Creative
half past	half back
half hour	half sister
half time	half brother
half moon	half heated
half dollar	glass half full
half a chicken	halfway there
half a pizza	halfway house
cut in half	half blood
half done	Subway Half Foot Sub
half price	two halves make a whole
half of the way	half pipe
half a minute	I'll go halves with you
give me a half	behalf
	halfback
	halftime
	halfway
	halfpenny
	half hearted
	halftones

71. Use the word "**full**" in as many ways as you can.

Common	Creative
full back	full scholarship
full tank	R. Buckminster Fuller
full moon	"A Spoonful of Sugar" - S
full grown	full gainer
full speed	Fullarton
full time	you're full of baloney
spoon full	full house
room full	full of praise
cup full	full stop
bucket full	handful
	glass half empty
	fully sick
	glass half full
	full cream milk
	playfully
	beautiful
	graceful
	thoughtful
	delightful

72. Use the word "**walk**" in as many ways as you can.

Common	Creative	
race walk	"Just Walk Away" - S	
slow walk	cat walk	Luke Skywalker
walking	Walk Against Want	Taylor Walker
go for a walk	walk of shame	Tyler Walker
walk the dog	talk the talk, walk the walk	
Walkers Flat	Paul Walker walking track	
walk around the block	"Walking on Sunshine" -S	
nature walks	"Walk 500 Miles" - S	Walkerville
sidewalk	walking trail	*Walk the Line - M*
walk to school	walking frame	
Walk the Dog yo-yo	walking the dog	
	"Walk the Dinosaur" - S	
	Walkie Talkie	
	Walk to School Day	
	Mega Sky Walk	
	Walking Dead	
	Frank Walker	
	Scarecrow Walks at Midnight - M	
	"Walking on the Moon" - S	

73. Use the word "**bus**" in as many ways as you can.

Common	Creative
bus pass	rhombus
bus stop	don't miss the bus
bus ticket	"Bus Stop" - S
bus lane	"Wheels on the Bus" - S
bus driver	busker
bus route	bust
London Bus	busting
Shuttle Bus	buster
Metro Bus	busting
City Bus	Magic School Bus
Big Red Bus	Magic Bus
	Venga Bus
	Des's Minibus
	business
	bustle
	hustle and bustle
	double decker bus
	abuse
	verbal abuse

74. Use the word "**train**" in as many ways as you can.

Common	Creative	
freight train	train of thought	trainload
passenger train	bridal gown train	eyestrain
train an employee	training wheels	
train for Olympics	camel train	
train station	ghost train	
train tracks	Sushi Train	
train lines	personal trainer	
train a dog	trainee	
steam train	trainer	
train crossing	strain	
electric train	strainer	
coal train	animal trainer	
	dolphin trainer	
	constrain	
	How to Train Your Dragon - M	
	"The Midnight Train to Georgia" - S	
	Throw Momma from the Train - M	
	Planes, Trains and Automobiles - M	
	drivetrain	

75. Use the word "**bike**" in as many ways as you can.

Common	Creative
push bike	biker
electric bike	biking
bike land	mountain bike racing
racing bike	on ya bike
mountain bike	Push Bike Song
bike stop	tandem bike
BMX bike	bike velodrome
new bike	motor bike racing
bike shorts	Bike Exchange
bike helmet	Bike Society
bike track	Bikers World
	Bikes are Us
	Biker Mice from Mars - M
	minibike
	bikeway
	bike lane

76. Use the word "**can**" in as many ways as you can.

Common	Creative	
garbage can	Canon	Candid Camera
oil can	candy	Canterbury
metal can	cannibal	can of worms
petrol can	canvas	canister
can of Coke	cancel	Candy Man
billy can	canteen	cannon ball
	candle	can't relate
	cancer	CanDo4kids
	pecan scans	
	how much can you bear	
	can can	Canon Camera
	Canada	Canberra
	Scandinavia	Beacon Lights
	incandescent	can't
	cane	American
	canasta	
	cannon	
	pelican	
	scandal	
	So You Think You Can Dance	

77. Use the work "**pot**" in as many ways as you can.

Common	Creative
flower pot	pot at end of rainbow
cooking pot	potassium
coffee pot	a watched pot never boils
	Harry Potter - M
crackpot	Potomac River
jackpot	Beatrix Potter
pot roast	despot
pot shot	spot
witches' pot	spotlight
teapot	pot in a poker game
pots and pans	pot of gold
pothole	pot black
clay pot	potter around
	pottery
	pot belly
	pot luck
	stir the pot
	potion
	spot

78. Use the word "**scrub**" as many ways as you can.

Common	Creative
scrub the floor	scrub the missile launch
scrub your hands	scrub the plan
scrub brush	scrubby terrain
scrub pots and pans	scrubby beard
back scrubber	scrubbing brush
outback scrub	scrubbed
scrub nature garden	Humbug Scrub
	scrubbing
	scrub the deck
	facial scrub
	scrubbable

79. Use the word "**cup**" in as many ways as you can.

Common	Creative
tea cup	hiccup cupcake
coffee cup	My Cup Runneth Over
Kings cup	buttercup
cup of tea	Stanley Cup
measuring cup	Davis Cup
gold cup	cup your hands
athletics cup	cupid
winners' cup	porcupine
	cheer up buttercup
	Adelaide Cup
	World Cup
	cup of soup
	chocolate cupcake
	cuppa
	tea cup ride
	"Build Me up Buttercup" - S
	cupboard
	eggcup
	occupant

80. Use the word "**pan**" in as many ways as you can.

Common	Creative	
saucepan	Peter Pan	bedpan
frying pan	pan for gold	claypan
pan fried	panel	pansy
pan for gold	pan handle	wingspan
dust pan	span	Pandora
dish pan	Wallspan	expand
	panda	frangipani
	panda cub	companies
	panel of judges	occupant
	panel beater	spangle
	selection panel	
	peer panel	
	wall panel	
	door panel	
	panel of a car	
	pants	
	pane	
	taipan	
	saltpans	

81. Use the word "**shoe**" in as many ways as you can.

Common	Creative	
shoe lace	If the shoe fits	shoeshine
sand shoe	shoe on the other foot	shoehorn
running shoe	walk a mile in my shoes	
shiny shoes	horseshoe	
pair of shoes	shoe shine boy	
	Spendless Shoes	
	Shoe Shed	
	one shoe, one boat	
	golden shoe	
	new pair of shoes	
	Old Woman Who Lived in a Shoe	
	"Diamonds on the Soles of my Shoes"- S	
	shoe horn	
	reshoe	
	sandshoes	
	shoelaces	
	shoestrings	
	shoemaker	
	snowshoes	

82. Use the word "**coat**" in as many ways as you can.

Common	Creative
coat hanger	coat of paint
final coat	coat with paint
ski coat	coating
first coat	chocolate coating
wear a coat	coat tails
lab coat	hat and coat
raincoat	coat of arms
light coat	fur coat
heavy coat	coat the outside
winter coat	Coates Hire
leather coat	undercoat
	overcoat
	topcoat
	petticoat
	sugar coated
	turncoat
	waistcoat
	bluecoats

83. Use the word "**hat**" in as many ways as you can.

Common	Creative	
wear a hat	hat parade	hate
top hat	hat party	what
safety hat	hats off	shatter
high hat	"Hats off to Larry" - S	phosphate
hat stand	*Hating Alison Ashley - M*	
hat box	chat backchat	
hard hat	rabbit out of the hat	hat pack
hat pin	high hat symbol	
	Mad Hatter	
	hatchet	
	hat trick	
	that	
	That's all folks	
	That's a wrap	
	hating	
	magician's hat	
	keep your hat on	
	"You Can Leave Your Hat On" - S	

84. Use the word "**stand**" in as many ways as you can

Common	Creative
witness stand	reach the standard
stand around	standard issue
stand trial	set the standards
taxi stand	standing room only
stand in line	Eastern Standard Time
hat stand	understanding
grand stand	stand of trees
fruit sand	Standish Bikes
news stand	standard of living
stand down	don't stand a chance
stand up	stand and deliver
hall stand	I have standards
	stand-up comedy
	Stand by Me - M
	Bandstand
	stand down
	standards
	stand up for the people
	standard weights and measures

85. Use the word "**sock**" in as many ways as you can.

Common	Creative
pair of socks	knock your socks off
odd socks	Bonds socks
wool socks	Nike socks
woollen socks	sock it to me
sock puppet	wind sock
	put a sock in it
	Joe Socks
	sockets
	socket set
	socks and jocks
	happy socks
	lucky socks
	Boston Red Socks
	White socks
	Robin socks
	power socket
	socket spanner
	TV socket
	toe socks

86. Use the word "**ball**" in as many ways as you can.

Common	Creative	
ball games	belle of the ball	snowball
soccer ball	ballroom	pinball
football	have a ball	
tennis ball	eyeball	
moth balls	*Strictly Ballroom - M*	
ball up	ball gown	
cricket ball	marbles	
fire ball	bawling your eyes out	
ball room	ballet	
hair ball	ballerina	
	ball boy	
	ballast	
	ballerina	
	balloon	
	softball	
	basketball	
	baseball	
	netball	
	ballistic	

87. Use the word "**bat**" in as many ways as you can.

Common	Creative	
cricket bat	battered	rebate
table tennis bat	flying bat	acrobat
fruit bat	bat sense	abattoir
beach bat	raise your bat	albatross
	"Bat out of Hell" - S	bathe
	Battle of Hastings	
	battlements	
	battle	
	batter	
	batting	
	battered fish	
	battering ram	
	wombats	
	numbats	
	battery	
	bathers	
	batik	
	battle	
	debate	

88. Use the word "**goal**" in as many ways as you can.

Common	Creative
goalie	goal attack
goal keeper	goal shooter
own goal	goal defence
short term goals	reach your goal
long term goals	score a goal
life goals	goals in life
line goal	ultimate goal
goal posts	find the back of the goal
goal umpire	goal wards
	goal tender
	goalless

89. Use the word "**stick**" in as many ways as you can.

Common	Creative
lucky stick	you're a stick in the mud I'll stick by you
gold sticks	marshmallow stick stick around
ice hockey stick	lipstick
fighting sticks	sticky date pudding
glue stick	sticky bun
	sticky fingers
	sticky tape
	stick to it
	walking stick
	stickers
	stick insect
	stick people
	stick finger
	stick man
	Sticky Notes
	sticky honey
	stick up a poster
	"Fix the Fence with Sticky Tape" - S
	sticks and stones may break my bones

90. Use the word "**club**" in as many ways as you can.

Common	Creative
football club	clubhouse
golf clubs	go clubbing
tennis club	nightclub
soccer club	club president
hockey club	club committee
lacrosse club	club secretary
sailing club	cave man club
book club	Culture Club
chess club	Mickey Mouse Club
social club	Saddle Club
dance club	Club Penguin
secret club	club someone
metal club	secret club
	club feet
	club man
	interclub
	super club
	clubrooms

91. Use the word **'sun'** in as many ways as you can.

Common	Creative
fun in the sun	sunscreen sunglasses
sun spot	sunrise sunbake
hot sun	sunshine eclipse of the sun
sun burn	fun in the sun sun bear
sun ray	"Here Comes the Sun" - S
sun light	"Sunshine Lollipops" - S
warm sun	"House of the Rising Sun" - S
hot sun	sunshade sun worshipper
sun hat	sundial sundried
sun dress	"April Sun in Cuba" - S
sun block	"Sunday Morning" - S
sun shower	Sunday
	sung
	Sunrise fruit
	Sunrise TV
	sunset
	Sunbury
	"A Little Ray of Sunshine" - S
	"You are the Sunshine of My Life" - S

92. Use the word **'water'** in as many ways as you can.

Common	Creative	
clear water	water wise	mouth watering
fresh water	Water world	waterbed
calm water	sacred water	watercraft
rain water	water purifier	underwater
flat water	Still waters run deep	watercolour
still water	waterfall	watertight
stagnant water	waterslide	break water
running water	water as far as the eye can see	
clean water	water on the brain	
flood water	water, water everywhere but not a drop to drink	
water plants	water down	
water lawns	water evaporation	
open water	water regulations	
salt water	water aerobics	
spring water	water ballet	
water bucket	waterproof	
	watermarks	
	water skiing	
	ground water	

93. Use the word **'beach'** in as many ways as you can.

Common	Creative
name of any beach	beached Beach Boys
Henley beach	beached whale beach bum
Brighton beach	storm the beach beach comber
public beach	a day at the beach beach buggy
nude beach	beach weather
local beach	Golden beaches
go to the beach	Beach House
beach towel	Beach road
beach wear	beach erosion
sandy beach	Beach patrol
private beach	We will fight them on the beaches…
rocky beach	beach picnic
beach ball	beach shack
beach shade	beach volleyball
beach bat	beach cricket
beach umbrella	surf beach
	Beachport
	"On the Beach" - S
	"Beach Baby" - S

94. Use the word **'one'** in as many ways as you can.

Common	Creative	
one day	just one minute	throne
one up	one fish, two fish	drone
one way	One Direction	tone
one object	one way street	phone
one chance	"One Call Away" - S	shone
	one upmanship	
	one size fits all	
	one in a million	
	"One Day when You're not so Pretty"- S	
	alone	
	"One is the Loneliest Number" - S	
	"One, Two, Three Four Five" - S	
	one million	
	World War One	
	one step at a time	
	one world	
	done	
	clone	
	"You're My Number One" - S	
	Military Two Step	

95. Use the word **'won'** in as many ways as you can.

Common	Creative
we won	wonder
won the race	Wonder Woman
won the prize	wonders of the world
won lottery	wonderful
won the game	"What a Wonderful World" - S
	"Wonderwall" - S
	Wonderland
	Winter wonderland
	Alice in Wonderland
	I wonder about the facts
	it's a wonder
	wonky
	wontons
	wondrous
	wondering
	wondered

96. Use the word **'double'** in as many ways as you can.

Common	Creative
double up	tennis doubles
double dip	double trouble
double scoop	double B truck
double play	stunt double
double bed	dirty double crosser
double date	double or nothing
double jointed	double choc
double chin	double mint
double exposure	on the double
double feature	double speak
double canoe	double down
double kayak	on the double
double scull	double play
double letter	Am I seeing double?
	redouble
	double think
	doublet

97. Use the word 'ten' in as many ways as you can.

Common	Creative
ten toes	ten out of ten attend
ten fingers	ten of the best listen
Ten Commandments	ten pin bowling kitten
count by ten	ten years in a decade tender
top ten	antenna Channel Ten
	she's a ten shorten
	often stencil
	bitten contend
	eaten intend
	frighten
	tent
	tenor
	tentative
	tenacious
	tentacles
	Tennis
	Network ten
	Number Ten Downing Street
	extend

98. Use the word 'sit' in as many ways as you can.

Common	Creative	
sit down	sit on it	visits
sit up	sitting room	sit-ups
sit on the chair	sitting room only	obesity
sit back	sit down at the front	density
sit at the back	please sit down	bedsit
sit in the front	site	campsite
sit still	building site	adversity
sit quietly	Internet site	curiosity
sit anywhere	transit	sitar
sit there	transit bus	
	transit corridor	
	transit lounge	
	sitter	
	baby sitter	
	house sitter	
	opposite	
	situation	
	transition	
	composition	

99. Use the word **'drum'** in as many ways as you can.

Common	Creative
drum kit	Drumsticks
drum set	drum solo
bass drum	drum roll
snare drum	drum it in
bongo drum	"Little Drummer Boy" -S
native drum	"Like a Drum" –S
oil drum	Drumsticks ice creams
ear drum	Dixie drum sticks
fire drum	Drummond Golf
kettle drum	Doldrums
	Can you hear the drums?
	chicken drumsticks
	drumming
	continuous drumming in your ears
	humdrum
	drumbeat
	conundrum

100. Use the word **'key'** in as many ways as you can.

Common	Creative	
to do with locking or unlocking	key to a map	smoky
house key	key to my heart	
car key	key idea	
door key	key question	
padlock key	key witness	
security key	key chain	
lost your key	key to the puzzle	
back door key	key note speaker	
bike key	monkey	
boat key	turkey	
diary key	donkey	
security key	hockey	
allen key	Hokey Pokey	
	jockey	
	keypad	
	keyboard	
	key cards	
	keystones	
	Mickey Mouse	

Section Two

---

101. Birds fly in the air. Name things that **fly**.

Common	Creative
any birds	clouds butterfly
any insects	ideas
flying saucers	insults
rockets	time
helicopters	bullets
jets	a fly ball
parachute	flying tackle
boomerang	to fly off the handle
gliders	flying buttress
balloons	fly by night operation
kites	Rocky the Flying Squirrel
bee	Dumbo the elephant
comets	trapeze artist
chickens	Superman
ducks	flags
	drones
	pilots
	plane passengers
	horsefly

---

102. You can catch a ball. Name things you can **catch**.

Common	Creative	
any ball	a cold	catch up
Frisbee	a show	a lift
boomerang	a plane	a sniffle
a pass	a bus	the flu
	a taxi	catch on
	your breath	
	your attention	
	catch your eye	
	a fish	
	a disease	
	headlice	
	dream catcher	
	"Catch a Falling Star" – S	
	a catchy tune	
	a thief	
	To Catch a Thief - M	
	rain in a bucket	
	catchy the game	
	Catcher in the Rye	

103. Cars are a popular form of transport. Name types of transport.

Common	Creative
buses	surfboard
trucks	roller skates
trains	roller blades
aeroplanes	skateboard
helicopter	travelator
bikes	hover board
tractor	monorail
Segway	rickshaw
go-kart	tuk tuk
scooter	dog sled
wheelbarrow	gondola
unicycle	paddleboat
boats	chairlift
tricycle	blimp
walking	time machine
running	lift
jogging	escalator
skipping	donkey
	fireman's carry

104. A fire alarm signals danger. Name types of signals.

Common	Creative
voice	radio
bells	television
siren	Wi-Fi
lights	Bluetooth
scream	smoke
shout	Morse code
whistle	dog bark
flags	body language
horn	running away
buzzer	finger pointing
traffic lights	loud speaker
signs	digital
alarm clock	scoreboard
lighthouse	flashing lights
	facial expressions
	wink
	sign language
	clap
	booing

105. A daisy is a garden flower. Name types of **flower**.

Common	Creative
rose	bunch of flowers
tulip	flower box
violets	flower child
sunflower	flower power
dandelions	Mayflower
geraniums	flower girl
pansies	bouquet
	Robbie Flower
	Pete Rose
	Daisy Mae
	Violet Crumble
	flowering plant
	wheat flour
	plain flour
	self-rising flour
	gluten free flour
	blossoms
	daisy chain
	Herb Douglas

106. Kangaroo Island is just off the coast. Name many **islands**

Common	Creative
any island	Treasure Island
Tasmania	Skull Island
Australia	"Islands in the Stream"- S
Hamilton	Ireland
Daydream Island	traffic island
Fraser Island	New York Islanders
King Island	pedestrian island
Long Island	oasis in the desert
Hawaiian Islands	kitchen island
Christmas Island	island ark
Norfolk Island	island bath
Ellis Island	chain of islands
	island railbird
	barrier islands
	oceanic islands
	continental islands
	volcanic islands
	Pacific Islander
	island atoll

107. Many people have dogs as pets. Name many pets

Common	Creative
any animal	crocodile
cat	falcon
fish	elephant
goldfish	petrol
rabbit	petroleum
guinea pig	petticoat
	petunia
	trumpet
	Muppet
	carpet
	petty cash
	petty larceny
	petal
	Peter Pan
	petrified
	Peter Alexander
	Pet Stock
	Pet Barn
	pet rescue

108. Most bands have a guitar player. Name many bands

Common	Creative
rock band	rubber band
Bandstand	wedding band
bandleader	headband
Rolling Stones	armband
Beatles	sweatband
Queen	wristband
Kiss	elastic band
Black Eyed Peas	bandage
The Vamps	band saw
Spice Girls	bandicoot
cover band	band of colour
	triangular bandage
	on the bandwagon
	banded pigeon
	concert band
	jazz band
	symphonic band
	orchestra band
	cover bands

109. Phar Lap was a famous horse. Name many horses

Common	Creative
palomino	horse sense
Clydesdale	horsepower
thoroughbred	horsing around
quarter	hoarse voice
Arabian	horseshoe crab
mustang	Horseshoe Bay
stock	horsefly
race	saw horse
stallion	"The Horses" - S
mare	horses for courses
pony	hold your horses
horse show	on ya horse
horseback	horse shoe
horse shoe	don't look a gift horse in the mouth
Black Beauty	don't put the cart before the horse
Trigger	straight from the horse's mouth
Secretariat	changing horse midstream
Sea Biscuit	as healthy as a horse
	flogging a dead horse

110. Oxygen is an important gas. Name many forms of gas

Common	Creative
hydrogen	indigestion
carbon	reflux
tear gas	gastric ulcer
natural gas	laughing gas
gas mask	gasket
gas station	gastropod
gas tank	Las Vegas
petrol tank	"Jumping Jack Flash is a gas gas gas" - S
gas range	gastro
gas cook top	Gasworks
gas fire	gastritis
gas heater	gasbag
gas hot water	flabbergast
Mobil	gasp
Shell	gash
Caltex	biogas
Liberty	gas monkey
gas pipeline	gas mask
gas lighting	gasoline

111. Cars have four wheels. Name things that have **wheels**.

Common	Creative
bikes	wheelie bin wheel alignment
motorbikes	freewheel flywheel
trains	Hot Wheels
Bus	spinning wheel
wheelbarrow	roulette wheel
wheel chair	Ferris wheel
Pram	cartwheel
shopping trolley	wheel and deal
roller skates	gears
Toys	big wheel in the business
lawnmower	Meals on Wheels
scooter	"Wheels on the Bus" - S
skateboard	wheels in motion
Cart	Wheels the magazine
limousine	mag wheels
wagon	Wheelworx
trolley	wheel and tyre package
	pinwheel
	waterwheel

112. A punch is a hit with a fist. Name many **hits**

Common	Creative	
Slug	hit and run	whiten
clobber	hit the nail on the head	architect
smack	hit the ceiling	hitched
Slap	hit the hay	whitewash
hit movie	hit list	white caps
hit song	hit the big time	
hit record	hit the high note	
	half hitch	
	hitch a ride	
	hitchhike	
	hit the jackpot	
	hit man	
	Adolf Hitler	
	"Hit Me Baby One More Time" - S	
	Hit the Road Jack - S	
	king hit	
	hit parade	
	white	
	hitched	

113. Pine is a type of wood. Name many **woods**

Common	Creative
maple	wooden
Oak	wooden horse
cedar	softwood
Teak	hardwood
wood lot	driftwood
wood carver	woodchuck
wood pile	blackwood
wood shed	Woodville
pulp wood	Norwood
	sawdust
	kindling
	woodwind instrument
	the woods
	Woody from toy story
	Woody Allen
	Woody Woodpecker
	Edward Woodward
	"If You Go Out in the Woods Today" - S
	wood worm

114. We use lights in the dark. Name many **lights**

Common	Creative
light bulbs	lighthouses
head lights	spotlight
traffic lights	lightning
light years	light weight
sun light	light as a feather
reading light	lighter than air
coloured lights	light beer
disco lights	light and easy
city lights	light fingered
night lights	light headed
glow sticks	light-hearted
fluorescent light	eggs over light
	I see the light
	"Blinded by the Light" - S
	"You Light up My Life" - S
	Lighting McQueen
	Gordon Lightfoot
	Green Lantern
	Charge of the Light Brigade - M

115. Farmers work the land. Name many **lands**

Common	Creative
land lord	England Holland
land owner	Greenland gangland
land developer	Finland parkland
landing field	Ireland wasteland
land mine	Thailand *Badlands - M*
landslide	Foodland gland
landscape	Alice in Wonderland
landlady	land of opportunity
	landslide election
	landlocked
	landmark
	landmark decision
	landing
	island
	"I Come from a Land Down Unde"r - S
	Neverland - M
	fantasy land
	mainland
	dockland

116. A bicycle has a chain. Name many **chains**

Common	Creative	
dog chains	supermarket chain	"Chain Reaction" - S
gold chain	chain of shops	
silver chain	daisy chain	
chain link	drag the chain	
chain link fence	chain of command	
door chain	chain lightning	
chain gang	chain stitch	
chain saw	chain smoker	
	chain reaction	
	chain letter	
	chain of events	
	Two Chains	
	"Unchain my Heart" - S	
	"Chain of Fools" - S	
	"Working on a Chain Gang" - S	
	Chain of Ponds	
	chain-smoker	
	chain wheels	
	chained	

117. The air is invisible. Name things that are **invisible**

Common	Creative
any gas	odours TV signals
gases	sound gamma rays
light	cold x-rays
wind	heat phone signals
transparent glass	love
ghost	hate
	greed
	pain
	The Invisible Man - M
	radio waves
	atoms
	antimatter
	ultraviolet light
	gravity
	infrared light
	magnetic fields
	electrons
	radar
	sonar

118. People like to have parties. Name kinds of **parties**

Common	Creative	
birthday party	Labour	party crasher
farewell party	Liberal	buck's party
going away	Republican	hen's party
welcome party	Democratic	
baby shower	search party	
pyjama party	party time	
wedding party	party plan	
end of year	party pies	
surprise party	party sausage rolls	
theme party	party favourites	
office party	party line	
costume party	party of two	
fancy dress	Mardi Gras	
garden party	Boston tea party	
after party	bridal party	
	bachelor party	
	bar mitzvah	
	masquerade	
	slumber	

119. Chefs make dishes. Name many **dishes**

Common	Creative
any cooking	dish lickers
any dining	dish out money
dog dish	tectonic plates
cat dish	home plate
satellite dish	a pretty women
	flying saucer
	dish out justice
	dish out punishment
	dish pan hands
	radish
	dishwashing liquid
	dishonourable discharge
	disharmony
	dishcloth
	dishearten
	dishevel
	dishonest
	dishonour
	dishwasher

120. A judge is in court. Name many **courts**

Common	Creative
volleyball	courting
basketball	courtyard
tennis	courtesy
netball	backcourt
court order	King's court
your day in court	courteous
settle out of court	courtesy
court martial	courthouse
people's court	courtly
lower court	courtroom
high court	courtship
supreme court	courtside
county court	forecourt
district court	frontcourt
court of appeal	discourteous
	courted
	"Court of King Caractacus" - S
	Court of King Arthur
	courtesan

Section Three

121. Name **groups** and what makes up the group. E.g. A herd is a group of cows

Common	Creative
animal or human groups	nonliving objects
band is a group of musicians	six-pack is a group of soft drinks
school is a group of fish	dictionary is a group of words
posse is a group of policeman	library is a group of books
crew is a group of sailors	bunch is a group of grapes
team is a group of horses	squadron is a group of airplanes
team is a group of players	armada is a group of boats
pack is a group of wolves	fleet is a group of ships
cast is a group of actors	batch is a group of biscuits
flock is a group of birds	constellation is a group of stars
brood is a group of chickens	host is a group of angels
murder is a group of crows	belt is a group of asteroids
stand is a group of flamingos	fleet is a group of cars
exaltation is a group of larks	network is a group computers
congregation is a group of magpies	bundle is a group of firewood
glide is a group of flying fish	battery is a group of guns
herd is a group of seahorses	chain is a group of islands
float is a group of tuna	string is a group of pearls
swarm is group of eels	stand is a group of trees

122. Name **starters** and say what they start. E.g. a key starts a car

Common	Creative
match starts a fire	ideas start a book
bell starts school	packing starts a trip
switch starts the TV	sunrise starts a day
button starts timer	jokes start laughter
wind starts a windmill	birth starts life
gun starts a race	CPR starts a heart
lights start the traffic	conductor starts music
capital letter starts a sentence	smiles start friendships
words start conversations	recipes start cooking
pen starts writing	jobs start earning
alarm starts the day	respect starts cooperation
steps start a walk	entrée starts a formal meal
siren starts a game	insults start an argument
	thread starts material
	ceremony starts Olympics
	snip starts a haircut
	go starts a race
	fire starts cooking
	seed starts a plant

123. Name **covers** and tell what they cover. E.g. horse blanket covers a horse

Common	Creative
spread covers a bed	reporter covers a story
tomato sauce covers spaghetti	thieves cover their tracks
syrup covers pancakes	mask covers a face
tablecloth covers a table	leaves cover the ground
rug coves the floor	teachers cover topics
paint covers wall	insulation covers the ceiling
lid covers a jar	tiles cover the roof
jumper covers torso	carpet covers the floor
carport covers cars	tiles cover the walls
socks cover feet	tarp covers a trailer
shoes cover socks	newspaper covers stories
hat covers a head	label covers a container
	plants cover the ground
	grass covers the backyard
	book covers information
	leather covers seats
	water covers the seabed
	skin covers the body
	chrome covers metal

124. Name **fasteners** and what they fasten. E.g. Buttons fasten shirts

Common	Creative
nails fasten timber	marriage joins people
zips fasten coats	butter fastens bread
hooks fasten clothes	anchor fastens a boat
tape fastens wrapping paper	hair ties fasten hair
pins fasten material	handcuffs fasten criminals
staples fasten papers	magnets fasten bills to fridge
blue tac fastens paper	lead fastens the dog
masking tape fastens rips	seatbelts fasten people
glue fastens joins	respect joins groups
string fastens packages	towbar fastens a trailer
	gate fastens safety
	locks fasten doors
	packaging fastens food
	emails fasten information
	security fastens safety
	fence fastens yards
	friendship fastens relationships
	cages fasten wild animals

125. Name **teachers** and what they teach. E.g. maths teachers teach division

Common	Creative
any school teacher	waiting teaches patience
any coach	sharing teaches thoughtfulness
art instructor	animal trainer teaches obedience
drama instructor teachers acting	books teach students
priest teaches religion	computers teach students
monks teach acceptance	parents teach their children
	practice teaches skills
	exercising teaches fitness
	hard works pays off
	give respect, get respect
	teamwork brings great rewards
	change is inevitable
	organisation is important
	mistakes help you learn
	failure makes you stronger
	opportunities are there to be taken
	good decisions lead to prosperity
	working together benefits everyone
	necessity teaches innovation

126. Name things that **absorb** and what they absorb. E.g. Sponge absorbs liquid

Common	Creative
towels absorb moisture	body absorbs nutrients
plants absorb sunlight	brain absorbs knowledge
bricks absorb paint	ears absorb sound
cotton absorbs liquid	sawdust absorbs spills
sponges absorb water	charcoal absorbs odours
dumps absorb waste	clothes absorb odours
clothing absorbs stiches	padding absorbs impact
	soil absorbs rain
	students absorb ideas
	dogs absorb training
	black holes absorb objects
	vacuum cleaners absorb dust
	filters absorb particles
	learners absorb information
	readers absorb literature
	mathematicians absorb numbers
	a decade absorbs years
	positive people absorb challenges
	banks absorb fees

127. Name things that **reflect** and what they reflect. E.g. mirrors reflect images

Common	Creative
mirrors reflect images	results reflect effort
water reflects backgrounds	decisions reflect thought
white reflects sunlight	good management reflects profits
dictionaries reflect meanings	age reflects appearance
blinds reflect heat	manners reflect upbringing
insulation reflects cold	timelines reflect history
roof reflects rain	standing ovation reflects admiration
banks reflect rivers	moonlight reflects atmosphere
buildings reflect weather	first impressions reflect opinions
	sunscreen reflects UV rays
	art reflects ability
	ability reflects training
	skills reflect practice
	cameras reflect moments
	clothing styles reflects fashion
	handwriting reflects neatness
	house designs reflect current trends
	food choices reflect taste

128. Name **tools** and who uses them. E.g. hammer is a tool of a carpenter

Common	Creative
hand tools used by professionals	couch is a tool of a psychiatrist
plane is a tool for a pilot	sunglasses are tools of lifeguards
voice is a tool of teachers	diplomacy is a tool for diplomats
scalpel is a tool of a surgeon	microphone is a tool for an announcer
lawnmower is a tool of a gardener	makeup is a tool for clowns
car is a tool of a racing driver	horse is a tool for a jockey
brushes are tools of a painter	ship is a tool for a sailor
spanner is a tool of a mechanic	ball is a tool for a footballer
stethoscope is a tool of a doctor	hoop is a tool for a basketballer
plunger is a tool of a plumber	bat is a tool for a cricketer
spices are tools of chefs	thermometer is a tool for a nurse
	microscope is a tool for a scientist
	computer is a tool for a researcher
	phone is a tool for a marketer
	dough is a tool for a baker
	money is a tool for a banker
	guitar is a tool for musicians
	tractor is a tool for a farmer
	scissors are a tool for a hairdresser

129. Name **producers** and what they produce. E.g. bike factory produces bikes

Common	Creative
tangible, concrete products	jokes produce laughter
McDonalds produce hamburgers	juries produce verdicts
clouds produce rain	teachers produce learners
sheep produce wool	coaches produce participants
cows produce milk	war produces misery
trees produce timber	sunburn produces pain
leaves produce oxygen	bites produce swelling
builders produce houses	practice produces champions
pulp produces paper	Apple produces iPhones
steel produces tall buildings	wine produces conversation
grapes produce wine	cakes produce celebration
plants produce flowers	jumpers produce warmth
hens produce eggs	shoes produce protection
	freezer produces ice
	ovens produce heat
	travel produces holidays
	rubbish produces waste
	rain produces rivers
	organisation produces results

130. Name types of **water** and tell where it is found. E.g. hot water is found in a bathtub

Common	Creative
salt water in oceans	frozen water in a glacier
falling water in a waterfall	water vapour in a cloud
running water in a tap	juicy water in a watermelon
cold water in a mountain stream	deionised water in an iron
soapy water in a washing machine	spring water in a bottle
bubbling water in a spa	water on the knee in an injured knee
flushing water in a toilet	carbonated water in a shop
waste water in a septic tank	icy water in the fridge
treated water in a sewerage pond	chlorinated water in a pool
	mineral water in a spring
	hot water in steam
	soft water in snow
	hard water in hail
	still water in dams
	conserved water in wetlands
	light water in clouds
	destructive water in storms
	storm water after heavy rain
	distilled water at a desalination plant

Section Four - Alphabet Words

1. Just Fruits

A	apples	apricot	avocado	
B	banana	blueberry	blackberry	boysenberry
C	currant	cherry	coconut	cranberry
D	date	dragonfruit	damson	
E	elderberry			
F	fig	feijoa		
G	grape	grapefruit	guava	gooseberry
H	huckleberry	honeyberry		
I				
J	jackfruit	juniper berry	jambul	jujube
K	kiwi fruit	kumquat		
L	lime	lemon	loquat	lychee
M	mango	melon	mulberry	mandarin
N	nectarine			
O	orange	olive		
P	peach	pear	plum	pineapple
Q	quince			
R	raspberry	rambutan	red currant	
S	strawberry	star fruit	satsuma	salak
T	tangerine			
U	ugli fruit			
V				
W	watermelon			
X				
Y	yuzu			
Z				

2. Vegetables Only

A	artichoke	asparagus	aubergine	alfalfa
B	beans	broccoli	bok choy	bean sprout
C	carrot	cabbage	celery	cauliflower
D	dill			
E	endive			
F	fennel			
G	green beans	garlic	ginger	
H	herbs	horseradish		
I	iceberg lettuce			
J	jalapenos	jicama		
K	kale	kohlrabi	kidney bean	
L	lettuce	leak	lentils	lima beans
M	maize	mushrooms	mung beans	Marrow
N	nettles			
O	onion			
P	pea	parsley	peppers	Parsnip
Q				
R	rhubarb	radish	rutabaga	
S	shallot	spinach	squash	split peas
T	turnip	tubers	taro	tabasco
U				
V				
W	watercress	wasabi		
X				
Y	yam			
Z	zucchini			

3. Show your colours

A	aqua	amber	apricot	azure
B	blue	black	brown	beige
C	cyan	cream	cobalt	copper
D	denim	dandelion		
E	emerald	eggplant		
F	fuchsia	flax	fern green	firebrick
G	green	grey	gold	goldenrod
H	harlequin	heliotrope	hollywood	
I	indigo	ivory		
J	jade			
K	khaki			
L	lime	lemon	lilac	linen
M	magenta	maroon	mauve	mustard
N	navy blue	navajo		
O	orange	olive	ochre	orchid
P	pink	purple	plum	puce
Q	quartz			
R	red	royal blue	rose	ruby
S	silver	scarlet	salmon	saffron
T	tan	teal	turquoise	terra cotta
U	ultramarine			
V	violet	vermilion		
W	white	wheat	wisteria	
X	xanthic			
Y	yellow			
Z	zucchini			

4. Animals on parade

A	anteater	antelope	alligator	alpaca
B	bear	bison	baboon	buffalo
C	cat	cow	cougar	cheetah
D	dog	donkey	deer	duck
E	elephant	emu	egret	elk
F	fox	flamingo	fowl	falcon
G	goat	goose	giraffe	gnu
H	horse	hen	hyena	heron
I	iguana	ibis	impala	insect
J	jabiru	jackal	jaguar	jackrabbit
K	koala	kangaroo	kite	komodo
L	lion	lama	leopard	lizard
M	magpie	monkey	moose	meerkat
N	numbat			
O	owl	otter	orca	ostrich
P	peacock	pelican	puma	penguin
Q	quail	quoll	quokka	
R	rabbit	rat	reindeer	raven
S	sheep	shrike	snake	stork
T	tiger	turtle	turkey	toucan
U	urial			
V	viper	vulture		
W	wallaby	warthog	wolf	whale
X				
Y	yak			
Z	zebra			

5. Car brands

A	Audi	Aston Martin	Alfa Romeo	Ariel
B	BMW	Bentley	Bugatti	Buick
C	Cadillac	Chevrolet	Chrysler	Citroen
D	Dodge	Datsun		
E				
F	Ford	Ferrari	Fiat	
G	GMC	General Motors		
H	Honda	Hyundai	Holden	
I	Infiniti	Isuzu		
J	Jaguar	Jeep		
K	Kia			
L	Lexus	Land Rover	Lamborghini	Lancia
M	Mazda	Mercedes	Mini	Mitsubishi
N	Nissan			
O	Opel			
P	Pagani	Peugeot	Porsche	
Q				
R	Renault	Rolls Royce	Ram	
S	Subaru	Saab	Suzuki	Skoda
T	Toyota	Tesla	TVR	
U				
V	Volkswagen	Volvo	Vauxhall	
W				
X				
Y				
Z	Zonda			

6. All Sports

A	athletics	archery	aquatics	acrobatics
B	bowling	bicycling	badminton	BMX
C	cricket	cycling	canoeing	court tennis
D	darts	dancing	dog racing	dodgeball
E	English billiards			
F	football	frisbee	fencing	futsal
G	golf	gymnastics	goalball	
H	handball	horse riding	hurdles	
I	ice hockey	ice skating	indoor skate	
J	judo	jump rope	jogging	jazz dance
K	karate	karting	kayaking	kung fu
L	lacrosse	lawn bowl	Luge	laser tag
M	marathon	martial arts	motor sport	
N	netball	ninpo		
O	outrigger	oz tag		
P	paintball	ping pong	pole vault	putt-putt
Q	quoits			
R	rugby	rowing	rodeo	roller skate
S	soccer	sailing	softball	surfing
T	tennis	table tennis	tai chi	t ball
U	unicycling			
V	volleyball	vaulting	vigoro	
W	wind surf	water polo	water skiing	wrestling
X	xc skiing			
Y	yoga			
Z	zorbing	Zumba		

7. Superheroes and Villains

A	Aqua man	Astro boy	Atlas	Ares
B	Batman	Buffy	Banshee	Blade
C	Cat Women	Capt Planet	Capt America	Capt Marvel
D	Darth Vader	Donatello	Domino	
E	Ego	Electro		
F	Flash	Falcon	Firestorm	
G	Gladiator	Goliath	Godzilla	
H	Hulk	Hercules	Han Solo	Hell Boy
I	Iron Man	Iceman	Indiana Jones	
J	Joker	James Bond		
K	Krypto	King Kong		
L	Lex Luther			
M	Marvel Girl	Medusa		
N	Nova			
O	Oracle			
P	Penguin	Phantom		
Q	Quantum			
R	Riddler	Rambo	Robin Hood	Ripcord
S	Superman	Shriek	Spider Man	Storm
T	Thor	Titan		
U	Ultragirl			
V	Venom	Vulcan		
W	Wolverine	Wonder Women		
X	X-man			
Y	Yoda			
Z				

8. Boys' Names

A	Andrew	Ashley	Anthony	Asher
B	Ben	Bruce	Bob	Bert
C	Colin	Clive	Cliff	Craig
D	Donald	Damien	Dane	Doug
E	Eric	Edward	Elvis	Ethan
F	Fred	Francis	Frank	Flynn
G	Gary	Graham	George	Greg
H	Harry	Harold	Henry	Hugo
I	Ian	Ivan	Isaac	Irvin
J	Jack	John	Joseph	Jacob
K	Keith	Kain	Karl	Ken
L	Lance	Larry	Leo	Lee
M	Mark	Malcom	Mario	Matthew
N	Neil	Nate	Nigel	Nick
O	Owen	Oliver	Oscar	Otto
P	Paul	Peter	Phillip	Pierce
Q	Quinton	Quincy	Quinn	Quinlan
R	Robert	Ralph	Ray	Reece
S	Steve	Sam	Scott	Shaun
T	Trevor	Thomas	Tom	Tim
U	Uri	Umar		
V	Vince	Victor	Vlad	Vincent
W	Wally	Warren	Wayne	Will
X	Xavier	Xavian		
Y	Yuri	Yosef		
Z	Zac	Zain	Zaid	Zavier

9. Girls' Names

A	Amy	Anthea	Anne	Aisha
B	Bella	Barbara	Belinda	Bethany
C	Carol	Catherine	Chloe	Cassie
D	Daisy	Dani	Dianne	Deanne
E	Eden	Edith	Ellie	Ellen
F	Faye	Felicity	Florence	Fiona
G	Georgia	Gina	Gemma	Gloria
H	Hanna	Hailey	Harriet	Hazel
I	Ida	Ingrid	Irene	Isabella
J	Jenny	Jade	Jane	Janet
K	Kaila	Karen	Kara	Kate
L	Lara	Leah	Leanne	Lucinda
M	Mary	Matilda	Meagan	Michelle
N	Nancy	Naomi	Natalie	Nicole
O	Olivia	Olga	Olive	Oriana
P	Paige	Patricia	Pauline	Pam
Q	Queen			
R	Rachel	Rebecca	Renee	Robin
S	Sandra	Sally	Susan	Sharon
T	Tania	Taylor	Tara	Tracy
U	Ursula	Ula	Una	
V	Vicky	Valerie	Veronica	Violet
W	Wendy	Wanda	Whitney	Winnie
X	Xena			
Y	Yasmin	Yvette	Yvonne	Yolanda
Z	Zara	Zoe		

10. Countries of the World

A	Australia	Austria	Argentina	Albania
B	Brazil	Bulgaria	Belgium	Belize
C	Canada	Chile	Chad	Cuba
D	Denmark	Dominica	Djibouti	
E	Egypt	Estonia	Ecuador	Ethiopia
F	France	Fiji	Finland	Faroe Is.
G	Germany	Greece	Ghana	Georgia
H	Hungary	Haiti	Honduras	
I	Italy	Iceland	India	Ireland
J	Japan	Jordan	Jamaica	
K	Kenya	Korea	Kuwait	Kiribati
L	Latvia	Libya	Lebanon	Laos
M	Mexico	Monaco	Malaysia	Maldives
N	Norway	Nepal	Nauru	Niger
O	Oman			
P	Poland	Portugal	Pakistan	Panama
Q	Qatar			
R	Russia	Romania	Rwanda	
S	Sweden	Spain	Switzerland	Syria
T	Turkey	Taiwan	Tibet	Tonga
U	Uganda	Ukraine	Uzbekistan	Uruguay
V	Vanuatu	Vatican City	Venezuela	Vietnam
W				
X				
Y	Yemen			
Z	Zaire	Zambia	Zimbabwe	

11. Occupations

A	actor	auditor	auctioneer	athlete
B	banker	baker	biologist	bricklayer
C	carpenter	caretaker	chemist	cleaner
D	doctor	dentist	disc jockey	driver
E	electrician	economist	ecologist	educator
F	fire officer	fencer	farmer	fisherman
G	gardener	geologist	goldsmith	guide
H	hairdresser	historian	herbalist	host
I	insurance	instructor	investment	investor
J	judge	jockey	joiner	jeweller
K	keeper			
L	lifeguard	lecturer	landscaper	lighting
M	manager	mechanic	midwife	musician
N	nurse	nanny	newspaper	nutrition
O	operator	optician	osteopath	
P	pharmacist	pilot	publisher	plumber
Q	quilter			
R	radio tech	referee	registrar	removalist
S	singer	sculptor	surgeon	solicitor
T	teacher	tiler	teller	tutor
U	usher	upholsterer	umpire	
V	veterinarian	valuer	valet	vicar
W	waiter	weaver	worker	woodcutter
X				
Y	youth work			
Z	zookeeper	zoologist		

12. Furniture

A	armchair	armoire		
B	bed	Bar	bench	bookcase
C	chair	cabinet	chest	couch
D	desk	dresser	divan	drapes
E	easy chair	end table		
F	footrest	Futon	footstool	folding chair
G	game table	garden bench	grandfather clock	
H	high chair	head board	hat stand	hammock
I	island			
J				
K	kitchen island			
L	lamp	lawn chair	love seat	lounge chair
M	mattress	mirror	mantel	
N	night stand			
O	ottoman	office chair		
P	patio chair	Pew	piano stool	park bench
Q				
R	rug	recliner	rocking chair	
S	seat	Stool	sideboard	sofa
T	table	throne	tea cart	trundle
U				
V	vanity			
W	wardrobe	water bed	work table	writing desk
X				
Y				
Z				

13. Clothing

A	apron	Attire	apparel	anorak
B	belt	Bib	button	boxers
C	cap	Coat	cape	cardigan
D	dress	Duds	diaper	drawers
E	earrings	earmuffs	evening gown	
F	frock	flip-flops	fedora	formal
G	gear	gloves	gown	glasses
H	helmet	hoodie	housecoat	headscarf
I				
J	jacket	Jeans	jumper	jodhpurs
K	knickers	Kilt	kimono	khakis
L	life jacket	leotard	leggings	lab coat
M	mittens	miniskirt	moccasins	muffler
N	nightgown	nightshirt	necklace	neckerchief
O	overalls	onesies	outfit	overcoat
P	pants	pyjamas	parka	poncho
Q				
R	raincoat	rugby shirt	robe	ring
S	sandals	shirt	skirt	singlet
T	tights	togs	top	t-shirt
U	uniform	underwear	undershirt	undies
V	vest	veil	visor	Velcro
W	waistcoat	wetsuit	waders	wig
X				
Y	yoke			
Z	zipper			

14. Musical Instruments

A	accordion	anvil	acoustic	alto sax
B	banjo	bell	bongo	bagpipe
C	castanets	cornet	cymbals	clarinet
D	drum	didgeridoo	dulcimer	double bass
E	electric guitar	euphonium	English horn	
F	flute	fiddle	fife	flugelhorn
G	guitar	gong	grand piano	glockenspiel
H	harp	harmonica	horn	harpsichord
I	instrument			
J	Jew's harp	jaw harp		
K	keyboard	kazoo	kettledrum	
L	lute	lyre		
M	maracas	mandolin	marimba	melodeon
N				
O	oboe	ocarina	organ	
P	piano	pan pipes	percussion	piccolo
Q				
R	recorder	reed	rattle	rainstick
S	snare drum	saxophone	sitar	string bass
T	triangle	trumpet	trombone	tuba
U	ukulele			
V	violin	viola	valve	vibraphone
W	whistle	woodwind	wind chime	washboard
X	xylophone			
Y				
Z	zither			

15. Boats

A	aft	astern	aloft	anchor
B	bow	boom	buoy	bilge
C	canoe	clipper	cruise	carrier
D	deck	dock	drift	dinghy
E	engine	escort ship		
F	fathom	ferry	fishing boat	freighter
G	galley	gondola	gunboat	gangway
H	helm	hull	hydrofoil	houseboat
I	inboard	ice breaker		
J	jet ski	junk	jib	jet boat
K	kayak	keel	ketch	knot
L	launch	lanyard	lifeboat	log
M	marine	mast	mooring	mariner
N	naval	nautical	navigate	navy
O	oar	onboard	overboard	offshore
P	paddle	PFD	porthole	punt
Q				
R	raft	rope	rudder	rowboat
S	sail	sailor	ship	stern
T	tack	tanker	tide	tug
U	u-boat			
V	vessel	voyage		
W	wake	warship	wheel	windward
X				
Y	yacht	yawl		
Z				

16. Tools

A	axe	anvil	allen key	adze
B	bevel	bellows	bolt	brush
C	chisel	crowbar	clippers	clamp
D	drill	drill bits	drill press	
E	edger	electric drill		
F	fastener			
G	glue	glass cutter	glue gun	grinder
H	handsaw	hacksaw	hammer	hone
I				
J	jig	jigsaw		
K	knife			
L	ladder	lathe	level	lever
M	mallet	mitre box	machete	measuring
N	nail	nut	nail gun	
O	o ring			
P	plane	pliers	pulley	plumb bob
Q				
R	rasp	router	ruler	rivet
S	screw	spade	square	stapler
T	trowel	tiller	tack	toolbox
U	utility knife			
V	vice			
W	wrench	wedge	wheel	workbench
X				
Y				
Z				

17. Computers

A	app	array	algorithm	analogue
B	bitmap	boot	bug	byte
C	clip art	cookie	compress	CD rom
D	domain	dot	download	drag
E	email	encrypt	enter	emoji
F	file	flash	freeware	firewall
G	graphics	gigabyte		
H	hardware	host	hack	hyperlink
I	inbox	icon	integer	internet
J	junk mail	java	joystick	
K	key	keyboard	keyword	
L	laptop	login	logout	link
M	monitor	modem	media	mainframe
N	net	network	notebook	
O	output	operating	online	offline
P	password	piracy	platform	path
Q	Qwerty	queue		
R	router	restore	reboot	ram
S	server	scroll	screen	scanner
T	toolbar	template	Trojan	terminal
U	URL	upload	undo	username
V	virus	virtual	version	
W	word	web	WWW	website
X				
Y				
Z	zip			

18. At the Beach

A				
B	barnacle	beach ball	boat	bikini
C	crab	coral	coast	currents
D	dune	dive	dock	dune buggy
E	ebb tide			
F	fish	flags	frisbee	fishing
G	gull			
H	hat	high tide	hermit crab	
I	island	ice cream		
J	jellyfish			
K	kayak	kelp		
L	low tide	life jacket	life guard	lake
M	mussels	mangroves		
N	neap tide			
O	ocean			
P	pelican	pier	palm tree	paddleboat
Q				
R	reef	rip	relax	
S	seagulls	shark	sunburn	surfboard
T	tide	towel	trunks	tsunami
U	undertow	umbrella	underwater	
V	volleyball	vacation		
W	wet	wharf	waves	whitecaps
X				
Y	yacht			
Z				

19. Weapons

A	ammo	arms	axe	arrow
B	baton	bomb	bullet	bazooka
C	cutlass	cannon	club	crossbow
D	dart	dagger	depth charge	
E	explosives	epee		
F	firearm	foil	flintlock	flail
G	gun	grenade	gunpowder	Gatling gun
H	hatchet	handgun	harpoon	howitzer
I				
J	javelin			
K	knife	katana		
L	longbow	lance	landmine	longsword
M	mace	musket	mine	mortar
N	nunchaku	nuclear	nerve gas	
O	ordnance			
P	pistol	pike	pickaxe	pepper spray
Q	quarter staff			
R	rifle	rocket	revolver	rapier
S	sword	sabre	spear	shotgun
T	tank	truncheon	trebuchet	taser
U	uzi			
V				
W	whip	weapon		
X				
Y				
Z				

20. Cooking terms

A	aerate	age		
B	bake	braise	blend	beat
C	cut	churn	chop	char
D	deep fry	drain	debone	dice
E	escallop			
F	fry	fillet	freeze	fricassee
G	grill	grind	garnish	glaze
H	heat	hash	hard boil	hull
I	infuse	ice		
J	juice	jell	julienne	
K	knead			
L	layer	leaven		
M	mix	mould	mash	marinate
N				
O	oven fry	overcook	oil	
P	pour	peel	pan fry	pickle
Q	quarter			
R	roll	rise	reduce	roast
S	skewer	slice	scallop	sieve
T	thicken	temper	trim	tenderize
U	unmould	uncured		
V				
W	whisk	whip	wash	wedge
X				
Y				
Z	zap	zest		

21. Hats off

A	Akubra	alpine hat		
B	baseball cap	bowler	beanie	beret
C	cap	crown	cowboy	chef's
D	dunce	derby	deerstalker	
E	equestrian	engineers		
F	fedora	fez	footy helmet	flat cap
G	glengarry			
H	helmet	hat	headdress	homburg
I				
J	jester	Juliette cap		
K	knit			
L				
M	mortar	mitre	motocross	
N	nightcap			
O				
P	pith helmet	panama	Pillbox	porkpie
Q				
R	rainhat	riding cap		
S	swim cap	straw hat	sun bonnet	sombrero
T	tiara	turban	top hat	ten gallon
U				
V	visor	Viking helmet		
W	witch's hat	watch cap		
X				
Y	yarmulke			
Z	zucchetto			

22. School

A	answer	atlas	arithmetic	assignment
B	book	binder	bookcase	backpack
C	crayons	compass	calendar	calculator
D	desk	dividers	dictionary	
E	exam	eraser	English	easel
F	folder	file	flash cards	flash drive
G	gym	glue	globe	glossary
H	homework	history	hole punch	highlighter
I	intelligence	interest	involvement	inquiry
J	Japanese			
K	keyboard			
L	language	library	lesson	laptop
M	maths	markers	maps	memorize
N	notebook			
O	organisation			
P	pencil	paper	pupil	project
Q	quiz	questions		
R	reading	ruler	recess	resources
S	students	science	scissors	sharpener
T	teacher	tape	test	thesaurus
U				
V	vocab			
W	whiteboard	writing	world map	watercolour
X				
Y	yardstick			
Z				

23. Art

A	abstract	airbrush	artwork	animation
B	brush	batik	blending	brightness
C	cartoon	canvas	charcoal	colour
D	decorate	draw	design	depict
E	easel	exhibit	etching	enamel
F	frame	fresco	film	form
G	graffiti	gallery	glaze	graphite
H	hue	hatching	highlight	
I	image	illustrate	ink	
J	junk art	jewellery		
K	kiln	kitsch		
L	line	landscape	lithograph	
M	media	mural	mosaic	marbling
N	nail art	naive		
O	oil paint	origami		
P	pencil	photo	pottery	print
Q	quilt	quill		
R	ruler	realism		
S	scale	sculpture	stencil	sketch
T	textiles	template	tone	tools
U	undertone			
V	varnish	visual		
W	watercolour	wax	woodcut	waterscape
X	xylography			
Y				
Z				

24. Family

A	ancestor	aunt	adoption	
B	brother	bride	bachelor	bridegroom
C	child	clan	cousin	caregiver
D	dad	daughter	descendant	divorce
E	engaged	estranged	eligible	ex wife
F	father	folks	friend	fiancée
G	grandpa	grandma	groom	genealogy
H	heir	husband	household	hereditary
I	infant	in law	inherit	identical
J	juvenile			
K	kin	kinship	kindred	kinfolk
L	lineage	loyalty	love	
M	mother	miss	mate	marriage
N	nephew	niece	newlywed	nuptial
O	offspring	orphan		
P	parent	partner	progeny	patriarch
Q	quads	quints		
R	related	relative	relations	
S	sister	son	spouse	single
T	tribe	twins	triplets	trust
U	uncle			
V	value			
W	wife	wedding	wedlock	
X				
Y	youth	youngster		
Z				

25. Body

A	arm	ankle	artery	abdomen
B	brain	blood	bone	back
C	calf	chest	cheek	chin
D	diaphragm	digestive		
E	eye	ear	elbow	
F	feet	finger	face	foot
G	glands	gums	groin	gallbladder
H	heart	hand	head	hair
I	instep	intestines	iris	immune
J	jaw			
K	knee	kidney		
L	leg	lips	lungs	larynx
M	mouth	muscle	molar	mandible
N	nose	neck	navel	nail
O	organ	ovary	oesophagus	
P	pupil	palm	patella	pore
Q				
R	ribs	radius	rectum	respiratory
S	skin	spine	skull	shoulder
T	toe	thumb	teeth	throat
U	ulna	uterus	urethra	urine
V	vein	vertebra		
W	wrist	waist		
X				
Y				
Z				

26. Time

A	afternoon	alarm	annual	anytime
B	before	bedtime	belated	biennial
C	clock	century	calendar	chronology
D	delay	day	decade	daylight
E	early	evening	eon	era
F	future	fortnight	fiscal year	
G	Greenwich			
H	hour	hands	half-life	high noon
I	in time			
J	jubilee	jiffy		
K				
L	late	leap year	lunar	
M	minute	month	morning	midnight
N	noon	now	night	nanosecond
O	on time	overtime	o'clock	
P	past	present	punctual	premature
Q	quarter hour			
R	recent	reset		
S	second	season	soon	sunrise
T	tonight	today	tomorrow	tardy
U				
V				
W	week	watch		
X				
Y	year	yesterday	yesteryear	
Z	zone			

27. Fish

A	anchovy	angelfish		
B	bass	blowfish	bull shark	barracuda
C	catfish	carp	clownfish	cod
D	dory	dragonfish	dogfish	darter
E	eel	emperor		
F	flounder	flying fish		
G	goldfish	garfish	grouper	guppy
H	hake	herring	haddock	halibut
I	icefish			
J	john dory	jackfish		
K	koi			
L	lungfish	lamprey		
M	mullet	minnow	marlin	mackerel
N	nurse shark	needlefish		
O	oarfish			
P	perch	pike	pufferfish	piranha
Q	quill fish			
R	roughy	ray	rockfish	
S	shark	stingray	snapper	salmon
T	tuna	trout	tiger shark	turbot
U				
V	viperfish	velvetfish		
W	whale	whiting	wrasse	
X				
Y	yellowtail	yellowjack		
Z	zebrafish			

28. Pirates

A	adventure	anchor	ahoy	ashore
B	barrel	brawl	buccaneer	bandanna
C	chest	crew	compass	cargo
D	dagger	deck	doubloon	daring
E	explore	escape	earring	eye patch
F	fleet	flag	first mate	fortune
G	galleon	gangplank	greed	gunpowder
H	heist	hull	hook	haul
I	island	illegal	infamous	
J	jewels	jolly roger	jetsam	
K	keel	knife	kidnap	kill
L	loot	lookout	lash	land
M	mutiny	mast	map	maroon
N	nautical	navigate	notorious	
O	ocean	outcasts	overboard	old salt
P	plank	parrot	pistol	plunder
Q	quest	quarters		
R	raid	rudder	rum	rigging
S	scurvy	sailor	shipmate	skiff
T	trade	treasure	tides	thief
U	unlawful			
V	vessel	vanquish	violent	vile
W	weapons	walk plank		
X	x marks the spot			
Y	yo-ho-ho			
Z				

29. Landforms

A	atoll	alluvial	archipelago	
B	bay	bluff	basin	beach
C	creek	crevasse	cave	cliff
D	delta	desert	dune	drift
E	equator	estuary	escarpment	
F	foothills	fjord	fault	falls
G	gorge	grotto	glen	gap
H	hill	headland	hollow	highland
I	islet	iceberg	island	isthmus
J				
K	knoll	knob		
L	lake	longitude	latitude	lagoon
M	mouth	mound	marsh	mainland
N	neck	narrows		
O	ocean	overhang	oasis	
P	pond	point	plain	peak
Q				
R	river	rock	rise	reef
S	seabed	slope	stream	shore
T	tableland	terrain	tributary	tundra
U				
V	valley	volcano	vent	vale
W	waterfall	wetland	watershed	
X				
Y				
Z				

30. Insects

A	ant	aphid	admiral butterfly	
B	beetle	bug	butterfly	bee
C	cricket	cicada	caterpillar	cockroach
D	dragonfly	dung beetle		
E	earwig	eggs		
F	fly	flea	fruit fly	firefly
G	grub	gnat	grasshopper	
H	hornet	horsefly	honeybee	housefly
I	imago			
J	June bug			
K	katydid			
L	Lice	larva	locust	louse
M	Moth	mosquito	maggot	midge
N	nymph			
O				
P	pond skater	pupa	praying mantis	
Q				
R	Roach			
S	stonefly	stink beetle	silverfish	scarab
T	termite	thrips	tsetse fly	
U				
V				
W	Wasp	weevil	waterbug	
X				
Y	yellowjacket			
Z				

31. Farm

A	acre	agriculture	animals	
B	bull	barley	bison	barn
C	cow	crops	chicken	cattle
D	duck	donkey	dog	dairy
E	ewe	eggs		
F	flock	fallow	feed	fruit
G	grains	goat	geese	gate
H	horse	herd	hatchery	harvest
I	irrigation	incubator	insecticide	
J	jersey cow			
K	kid			
L	lamb	land	longhorn	llama
M	meadow	mare	milk	mulch
N				
O	oats	orchard	ox	
P	produce	poultry	plant	pig
Q				
R	ripe	ram	rabbit	ranch
S	stable	silo	sheep	scarecrow
T	tractor	trough	turkey	tiller
U	udder			
V	vegetables			
W	wheat	windmill	water	weeds
X				
Y	yak			
Z				

32. Maths and Numbers

A	addition	answer	average	axis
B	binary	billion		
C	circle	cube	curve	coordinates
D	decimal	degree	divide	dozen
E	ellipse	equation	even	exponent
F	formula	fraction	factor	five
G	graph	geometry	greater than	
H	half	hypotenuse	hundred	hundredth
I	integer	inequality	inverse	isosceles
J				
K	kilo			
L	line	long division	linear	less than
M	mean	median	multiply	minus
N	negative	numerator	numeral	null
O	obtuse	odd	octagon	ordinal
P	plus	percent	plane	product
Q	quarter	quotient	quadrilateral	
R	rectangle	rounded	radius	rhombus
S	solve	sum	symbol	sphere
T	times	tangent	triangle	trapezium
U	unit			
V	variable	vertex	volume	
W	whole			
X	x-axis			
Y	y-axis			
Z	zero			

Use a list to answer letter questions. New themes.

	Starting with _			Starting with _
1	A suburb		1	5 letter word
2	Cold things		2	In the fridge
3	Breakfast foods		3	Street names
4	TV shows		4	Parts of the body
5	Appliances		5	Birds
6	Drinks		6	Things you replace
7	Famous people		7	Sandwiches
8	Desserts		8	World leaders
9	Found on a map		9	Excuse for being late
10	Athletics		10	Ice cream flavours

	Starting with _			Starting with _
1	TV stars		1	Celebrities
2	Things that jump		2	Reptiles
3	In a park		3	Parks
4	6 letter word		4	Leisure activities
5	Gemstones		5	Allergic to
6	Sticky things		6	Famous characters
7	Awards		7	Menu Items
8	Spices		8	Types of iollies
9	Bad habits		9	What you hide
10	Go shopping for		10	Nicknames

	Starting with _			Starting with _
1	In the sky		1	Gifts
2	Pizza toppings		2	Things that are black
3	Afraid of		3	In your purse
4	What you measure		4	World records
5	Book titles		5	Hobbies
6	Restaurants		6	People in uniform
7	Medicines		7	In the park
8	Toys		8	At the circus
9	7 letter word		9	Made of plastic
10	Computer game		10	Do with friends

Neil Wuttke Biography

I have been a Primary School teacher for the past 42 years, predominately working with Middle School children aged 11 to 13.

For the last 26 years, I have been an active participant in the Tournament of Minds Competition and adapted and developed my teaching style to suit creative thinking and problem solving as an embedded practice.

In 1994, I joined the committee of the Tournament of Minds and as part of my committee role, have facilitated training and development workshops for students and teachers motivating and helping them to develop creative thinking strategies and practices in the classroom.

Over the last three years I have been the Co-Director of the South Australian branch of the Tournament of Minds. I have been a national judge for more than twenty years.

During this time, I have been continually asked for information and resources that can support teachers in the classroom to initiate and develop brainstorming techniques that lead to independent thinking.

It has been a passion of mine to help students develop higher order thinking skills and be able to solve complex problems. Many teams that I have facilitated to do the Tournament of Minds competition have gained Tournament Honours and in 2015 one of my teams won the State Final.

Through my wide experience, teaching in a wide diversity of schools, I have proven that students from any school, no matter what the socio-economic background can achieve significant results if given the opportunity and experience.

I certainly enjoy having fun when working with students to improve their creative thinking ability and problem solving abilities. It is a positive experience watching them develop confidence in their divergent thinking.

I live in the South-Western suburbs of Adelaide and teach at Henley Beach Primary School. My other passions include working as a volunteer at my local football club and coaching football at junior district level and being involved in all water sports. I have been involved with Vacswim as the Instructor in Charge for the last 45 years.

LOADING IDEAS

Printed in the United States
By Bookmasters